Respect the Image

There are Christian resources on communication in human relationships that tell the reader lots of stories but fail to connect these practical anecdotes, challenges, and instructions to biblical truths that transform the heart. On the other hand, there are resources that tell the reader eternal truths about conducting relationships as God intended but that leave the reader with little in the way of procedural knowledge—with no practical answers to "How do I do that?" *Respect the Image* helps us all precisely because Tim aims to make every truth transformative and every story connect to the truth.

—**Jeffrey S. Black**, Professor and Chair of the Department of Counseling and Psychology, Cairn University; Director of Counseling Services, Oasis Counseling Center, Cairn University

In *Respect the Image,* Tim Shorey reminds us of the importance of being engaged listeners who seek authenticity and love genuinely as a pathway to peace with our neighbors. With biblical insight and personal transparency, Tim provides effective, practical steps to pursuing peace with those with whom we might disagree. Requiring truth-telling and vulnerability, while recognizing the full humanity of others, and embracing both our uniqueness as well as our unity in Jesus Christ as an image of the gospel, *Respect the Image* is a focused and helpful plea for greater listening and learning in all our relationships.

—**Ruth Naomi Floyd**, Vocalist; Director of Jazz Studies, Cairn University; Lecturer on African-American Spirituals and Resident Artist, Temple University

The introduction to this book is exceptional and will serve people on many levels, and the entire work is deeply theological and gospel saturated. Its applications are clear and well connected to the truths that it presents. And the writing is winsome. Although the author presses into areas that can be challenging for people, he does so with a pastoral tone and without any harshness. I would recommend this book and use it for my leadership small group (as well as any other group). It will serve the church well.

—**Kyle Huber**, Lead Pastor, Greentree Church, Egg Harbor Township, New Jersey

Expertly crafted, this rich biblical treatment of relational and racial unity is a blessing and an encouragement. Tim challenges us to see and respect the image of God in everyone—those who are like us and those who are not like us. This is a high and holy calling that, if every believer heeds it, will glorify the one true God and bring change to our homes, communities, churches, and nation. Here is a practical book to read often and practice always.

—**Diane Hunt**, Counselor; Editor and Coauthor, *Crossing the Jordan: Living Victoriously in Difficult Relationships*; Conference Speaker

As I read this powerful and riveting book, I found myself confronted by sound theological truth that was laid out in plain, easy-to-understand language. I got no further than the first chapter before I was confronted by the bold truth Tim had penned. His winsome style of writing drew me in, making it easier for me to receive Spirit-filled correction and admonition on how I speak to others—beginning at home! This should be a sermon series for churches across our nation!

—**Anthony W. Hurst Sr.**, Part-time Professor, School of Divinity, Cairn University

In *Respect the Image,* Tim Shorey provides the glasses we need in order to see people as God does and to love and honor them for who God made them to be—image bearers of the King. Shorey offers young and old, single and married, and people of all backgrounds a compelling biblical pattern for living life in relationship with one another. Get this book, read it, and live it out—you won't be disappointed.

—**Marty Machowski**, Pastor; Author, *The Ology: Ancient Truths Ever New* and *Long Story Short: Ten-Minute Devotions to Draw Your Family to God*

Respect the Image is a winsome, creative, and biblically faithful book that was a pure joy to read. Shorey does an excellent job of compelling the reader to grow spiritually in the important area of communication and to realize the spiritual significance of doing so. The book addresses how communication impacts racial, social, and political tensions as well as giving us practical ways to move forward with hard conversations. *Respect the Image* is one of the best books I've read this year, and I have already commended it to my church family.

—**Mike Seaver**, Lead Pastor, Risen Hope Church, Summerville, South Carolina; Founder, *1Charleston*

RESPECT THE IMAGE

REFLECTING HUMAN WORTH IN HOW WE LISTEN AND TALK

TIMOTHY M. SHOREY

P&R
PUBLISHING
P.O. BOX 817 • PHILLIPSBURG • NEW JERSEY 08865-0817

Italics within Scripture quotations indicate emphasis added.

Printed in the United States of America

Library of Congress Cataloging-in-Publication Data

Names: Shorey, Timothy M., author.
Title: Respect the image : reflecting human worth in how we listen and talk / Timothy M. Shorey.
Description: Phillipsburg, New Jersey : P&R Publishing Company, 2020. | Includes bibliographical references. | Summary: "All people are God's image-bearers . . . but so often we treat one another like weasels, not wonders. Shorey's Bible-based answer is the COMMUNICATE lifestyle-transforming relationships and lives"-- Provided by publisher.

Identifiers: LCCN 2019048199 | ISBN 9781629957128 (paperback) | ISBN 9781629957135 (epub) | ISBN 9781629957142 (mobi)
Subjects: LCSH: Interpersonal relations--Religious aspects--Christianity. | Respect for persons. | Theological anthropology--Christianity. | Communication--Religious aspects--Christianity.
Classification: LCC BV4597.52 .S565 2020 | DDC 241/.697--dc23
LC record available at https://lccn.loc.gov/2019048199

To my multicolored and multicultured
Risen Hope Church family.

In complexity, adversity.
In adversity, humility.
In humility, charity.
In charity, unity.
In unity, fidelity.
In fidelity, beauty.
In beauty, doxology.

CONTENTS

FOREWORD

Imagine a man working in a dark mine. All day long he tosses aside worthless rubble. But if he discovers the glint of a carbon crystal among the other stones, his whole outlook will change instantly . . . assuming, of course, that he is aware that a diamond is in his grasp. Without this knowledge, he will see only rocks.

Too often we fail to see that the people around us are diamonds in the rough. We need help with recognizing the priceless treasure of every person. Not only will having this understanding keep us from tossing others aside like so much rubble, but, as Tim Shorey argues, it will also change the way we communicate with them on a daily basis.

Tim has written this book to reintroduce us to the image bearers whom we walk and talk with every day. And he helps us to ensure that the words we speak are worthy of the royalty we are addressing. God created each of us in his image to reflect his glory—even those who reject their inheritance as sons or daughters of the King. Tim helps us to see that words are a precious commodity with which we can either build up or tear down. When we use them to build up, we reflect the image of God in us. When we use them to tear down, we cast a shadow over that image.

When we lose sight of the special ways in which we each reflect our Creator, the love that should be a part of our communication is often next to go. *Respect the Image* provides a recipe for restoring communication that honors God by honoring the image of God in man. When put into practice, the instruction in these pages has the power to transform our relationships. Tim offers the reader "a complete life makeover" and introduces "a whole new way to live" (see p. 18).

You may think that those are bold claims, but I've seen Tim embody this in his own life. I've watched him love those who have tossed aside the value of a godly relationship with him in order to become his enemies. I've seen him give of himself in order to serve an ethnically diverse congregation and adjust his communication in order to better care for folks who have differing cultural backgrounds. Tim is looking forward to heaven, where people of every tribe and tongue will stand shoulder to shoulder in shared praise and unified communication. He believes that our diversity reflects God's image more fully than any homogenized view of humanity does.

Tim lifts our understanding of people to a higher level. Even though "we are immortals traveling through life with immortals [and] eternal splendors conversing with eternal splendors" (p. 27), when our gaze is weighed down by our sinful nature, we miss the incredible worth of the lowest of men. If we should see them for who they are—bearers of the heavenly seal and reflectors of the majestic creator—then we would surely speak to them with honor. Even if they are a nagging neighbor, an incredulous boss, or, even worse, an enemy, we can communicate with people with grace, peace, humility, and love.

Let me invite you to join Tim on this journey. He would say that he has plenty to learn—more ground to cover. But he's further down the path than I am—and perhaps than you are, as well. Read this book and welcome it like the voice of a traveling companion who is shouting, "I've found the path!" amid a thick, dark forest in which you have both been lost.

While *Respect the Image* is a treasure of truth and wisdom, Tim's writing is full of practical suggestions and illustrations that are designed to help you to grow in effective, godly communication. Apply the lessons he has provided, and the folks you are close to will notice. Tim is a pastor, and that shines through these pages—while he wants you to learn, he even more so wants you to grow. I have grown watching Tim practice the truth he's written about in these pages—and am the better for it. I'm glad that, through the pages of this book, you get to share the friend and pastor I have come to know and love.

Marty Machowski
Pastor and Author

PREFACE

CHOOSING OUR VOWEL CAREFULLY

What happens when two people meet over coffee or come face-to-face in conversation or in conflict? Here is a still more pressing question: what *should* happen? Are there *oughts* and *ought nots* that should govern how we listen and talk? The answer that we choose hinges on what we think it means to be human. In fact, how we define humanness will decide the quality of every relationship in our lives.

In simple terms that everybody can understand, our options appear to be three. Humans may be *chimps*—no more than accidental evolutionary cousins to tree-swinging primates. If so, we can and will relate to others as we'd relate to the orangutan on a safari or the back alley rodent that is scouring through refuse for dinner. Humans may be *chumps*—no more than thickheaded, messed-up, seriously damaged moral and relational misfits. If so, we can and will relate to others as we relate to things that are broken beyond repair: by throwing them all away until we find one that works to our liking for a while. Finally, humans may be *champs*—created beings who are made to bear God's image, transcend moral mediocrity, rule the earth, and inhabit eternity. If so, we can and *must* relate to others as we would relate to cosmic royalty—with nothing but respect.

Although only a single letter separates each of these options, they represent vastly different views of life and of what it means to be *us*. Everything good in human relationships depends on whether we choose the right vowel. As this book will argue, we are not chimps; though there is no denying that, due to cosmic rebellion and sin, we are spiritual and moral chumps. But, at the same time, we are much more than chumps. We are made to be champs—immortal sin-conquering and world-ruling victors.

Despite all our human failings, there is a word-defying quality about humanness that should be seen and known and felt. Each person exudes a beauty that is tinged with glory. Every human on the planet is a being that is worthy of wonder—an immortal who is poised on the cusp of eternity. As crusted with sinful grime as we might be, we are all divine icons and earthly images of the heavenly; we all have stories to tell and glories to share.

WHO THIS BOOK IS FOR

I have written this book to show how profound respect matters when we encounter one another on the countless battlefields of life. It is the fruit of thirty-seven years of pastoring that have included around fifteen thousand hours of counseling and thousands more hours of studying the Scriptures, reading about relationships, dialoguing across cultural and racial lines, and simply being with people. My experience tells me that what God says about human relationships and communication is for people of all ages and stages. More specifically, it's for

- anyone who isn't a hermit;
- spouses who want to bond and become one;
- parents who want to navigate the minefield of their teens' adolescence without losing life or limb in the process;
- siblings who have turned their home into a Civil War Gettysburg;

- pastors who want to lead humbly, as well as congregations who want to follow in kind;
- pastoral teams who want to serve together with effectiveness and trust;
- bosses and workers who don't want the workplace to be a war zone;
- the white, the black, the brown, and the officer in blue who deeply misunderstand and cynically distrust one another;
- the liberal and the conservative who care deeply about the same things but find it hard to believe that they do;
- people who are trying to share community life—whether in the hood, in a rural town, or elsewhere—without tearing one another's eyes out.

This book will not address all the issues and conflicts that people may face. But it will address *how* to address them—and that, I believe, is what is needed most.

THEOLOGICAL FOUNDATIONS

Let me set expectations. *Respect the Image* is part theology—a study of God. It is part anthropology—a study of humans. And it is part methodology—a study of principle and practice. It is a truth and life blend: doctrinal and practical theology in the same mix. Three great foundational truths undergird the practical teaching of this book:

1. *God talks and listens.* God reveals himself in love and holiness and hears us in all our weakness, longing, need, and love. This truth dignifies and sanctifies communication. To communicate is to be godlike; to communicate *well* is to be godly.
2. *Humans are made in the image and likeness of God.* As the "offspring" of God's being, we are immortals conversing

with fellow immortals. Consequently, we should reflect the image that we bear and respect the image that we share.

3. *In all our communication efforts, we need gospel assurance.* Our comfort is grounded in the atoning death and perfect righteousness of Christ, which are both counted as ours through faith in him alone. Without this blessed assurance, guilt, regret, and insecurity will crush our spirits, stymie our communication, and leave our relationships in the shallows—if not in the grave.

The first of these truths inspires our worship and trust. The second honors those who bear the image and elevates our discourse. The third answers our guilt and produces confidence for the way ahead.

PECULIARITIES, ILLUSTRATIONS, AND CAVEATS

Built on these theological foundations, this book includes eleven principles acrostically arranged. The word *COMMUNICATE* will guide us through these principles as we encounter them in the book, with a bit of simple poetry and alliteration added in to help to secure truths in place. These devices have a long history as well as a biblical precedent, and I use them to help to hook truths into minds and hearts.[1] My acrostic is longer than most, simply because relationships require a comprehensive life change that is guided by many different precepts and truths. But it can still aid your memory and produce a GPS when your relationships leave you lost and confused. When that happens, the eleven biblical principles it contains, if empowered by the Spirit

1. Not everyone prefers alliteration. Yet even so esteemed a theologian as J. I. Packer explains his use of alliteration as "a preacher's ploy for pointedness. Pardonable? Perhaps." J. I. Packer, *Keep in Step with the Spirit: Finding Fullness in Our Walk with God* (1984; repr., Grand Rapids: Baker Books, 2005), 40.

and committed to memory—and, even more, to life—can make a mighty big difference.

Reader release: if you cannot (or choose not to) remember my memory device, forget about it. No harm will be done; no offence taken. And as for the poetry? It is a simple attempt to secure things in place a little more snugly. If it doesn't work for you, it too may be freely ignored.

I should add as well that all the stories throughout this book are true unless I indicate otherwise. I have changed names and added circumstantial details to protect identities without embellishing the facts. Quotations are either reproduced verbatim or accurately summarized. Likewise, the actions that are described are honest representations of what I have seen, heard, or read.

Finally, I have included quotations whenever I think them helpful. Quoting people is problematic, however, in that I'm quoting *people*. More than a few have been guilty of, or party to, some bad theology or politics or morality, to go along with whatever good they may have said or done. If I quote someone on one point, it doesn't mean I agree with him or her on every point. I almost certainly do not.

A WHOLE NEW WAY OF LIFE

This book is about life change.

Years ago, I counseled a couple who were on the brink of divorce. Theirs was an angry, loveless marriage, taped together by the couple of kids they shared. Children often keep rickety families together and afloat for a while; but in this case, the mess that Dad and Mom brought into my office was a perfect storm that was about to blow it all to oblivion. Their problem was an utter breakdown of communication. They had no idea they had each married an image bearer—an offspring of God. And, having no respect for the image, they had no clue how to converse with the immortal human being with whom they were living.

I took a few sessions to lead them to God, to the gospel, and to the COMMUNICATE principles in this book, drawing from the Word, from life, and from my own personal messed-up experiences. I have never forgotten the wife's pensive pause when I finished my counsel to them. Clearly she was crafting a careful response, which finally came: "Tim, what you are asking us to do is a complete life makeover. This is a totally different lifestyle than we've lived to this point. I mean it. It's a whole new way to live."

She was right. Godlike love isn't half-in. It goes after it all—whole and hard. If we really want profound respect and joyful love to mark our relationships, then we'll have to buy into something more than three easy steps. We'll need a complete heart makeover—a whole new way to live.

You will discover a love- and hope-producing message in the pages that follow. I pray that it will provide the help that you need to live life in a whole new way—to listen, to learn, to lament, to laugh, to love, and to linger, all in relationship with the people with whom your life intersects. These are the graces that make our human-to-human connections truer and deeper—the very things that make us like the God in whose image we are made.

ACKNOWLEDGMENTS

Thanks are more than due to all those who have helped this book become a reality.

Thanks to Nancy Difabio, who first encouraged me, when I was still a very young pastor, to take this material into the world—to public high school seniors.

Thanks to Rush Witt, Amanda Martin, Dave Almack, and the whole P&R team, who caught a vision for *Respect the Image* and were willing to look beyond the risks posed by an unknown author.

Thanks to all those who helped to preview my manuscript and sent along all kinds of helpful suggestions: Ron Woudenberg, Nykki Effunuga, Kyle Huber, Mike Seaver, Marty Machowski, Ethan Shorey, Rob Saathoff, Ruth Naomi Floyd, Diane Hunt, Anthony Hurst, Vincent Callaway, and Jeff Black.

Thanks to Risen Hope Church—the church family with whom I get to do life and love; the friends and family in faith who have hung close and tight, despite the challenges of the journey.

Thanks to Leo Parris, Alex Chen, Rick Butler, Jared Mellinger, Andy Farmer, and Marty Machowski, who have all encouraged me often to do some writing.

Thanks to all my children, by blood and marriage, whom I love more than life and who have filled my life with joy.

Thanks to all the grandkids, who have promised never to forget that I love them.

And thanks to Gayline—my dearest treasure on earth—who has loved me and cheered me on, even from pretty ancient times. There is simply no one on earth I would rather listen to and talk with than you. Thanks for living this book with me.

INTRODUCTION

GOD, THE IMAGE, AND THE GOSPEL

"And God said . . ." (Gen. 1:3)

"You have . . . crowned [us] with glory and honor." (Psalm 8:5)

Since it's God's image we reflect,
Let us converse with deep respect.

Readers tend to be in a hurry, especially if they are in the middle of a mess. I get it. If I have broken plumbing and the house is flooded, I'm not interested in opening a homeowner's manual to a ten-page introduction called "The Philosophy of Pipes and Drains." If water is where water shouldn't be, and if stuff is coming up that should be going down, I want to know how to turn off the water, clear the pipes, and get it fixed.

You may have picked up this book in order to find a quick fix. But while you will find much practical help throughout its chapters, you should know that no true and lasting fix can happen unless we start with what we believe and work from there. To be blunt, the reason why our relationships are broken and our communication pipes are making stuff come up that should go down is because the theological pipes through which our communication flows are both misaligned and backed up all the way to the street. Fast-acting drain cleaner won't help this.

Communication is a theological exercise before it is a relational one. When you and I interact, we apply our up-to-this-very-second core beliefs. Thus, *bad* communication is a result of poor or unapplied theology, which leads to fractured families, racial tensions, class warfare, church splits, neighborhood war zones, and international crises. And *good* communication is a conscious application of what we know about God, what we know about humans, and what we know about the gospel—all of which leads to respect, healing, peace, and love.

Before we gather tools to improve our communication techniques, we need to understand three key communication-related truths. In the process of doing so, we will discover that truth transforms. The fix begins before we even pick up a tool.

TRUTH ONE: GOD SPEAKS

Calvin can help us with the theology part of this. Not to disappoint my Reformed friends, but I'm referring to a certain six-year-old Calvin of comic strip fame rather than to the sixteenth-century Calvin of Protestant Reformation fame. Those in the know will realize that while sixteenth-century Calvin planted theological TULIPs with care, six-year-old Calvin was more likely to uproot his mom's tulips in mischievous fun. However, Calvin the Younger sometimes speaks for humanity when he philosophizes. For example, when conversing about the Christmas mystery of Santa Claus with Hobbes, his stuffed tiger, six-year-old Calvin expresses skepticism about God.

> Calvin: "This whole Santa Claus thing just doesn't make sense. Why all the secrecy? Why all the mystery? If the guy exists, why

doesn't he ever show himself and prove it? And if he *doesn't* exist, what's the meaning of all this?"

Hobbes: "I dunno. . . . Isn't this a religious holiday?"

Calvin: "Yeah, but actually, I've got the same questions about God."[1]

That's some very bad Calvinism there. Young Calvin thinks that God has cloaked himself in secrecy—which is ironic, given that in the strip, he complains about a silent God while frolicking outside in a world that proclaims God's glory (see Ps. 19:1). The Creator shows himself every day through all the galactic and microscopic wonders he has made—ensuring that his existence and character can be seen clearly by all (see Acts 14:17; Rom. 1:19–20). In addition, he has planted a "you-know-that-I-exist" seed inside all of us—writing his truth upon, and shining his light into, every heart (see John 1:1–9; Rom. 2:15).

Still more ironic is that Christmas, the context for young Calvin's philosophizing, is all about God's showing himself in the flesh. As true as it is that God has spoken for a long time through nature and Scripture, in these last days he has spoken to us through his Son (see Heb. 1:1–3). Jesus of Nazareth is God in a body—God's breathtaking, perfect, eternal divine image revealed. He is God's *here-I-am* and *who-I-am*, delivered to the human race.

God has shown himself and spoken to us so clearly that no one has any excuse for not knowing him. The problem with young Calvin (the same problem that is shared by most humans) is that he is so busy listening to his own voice—and causing general mayhem—that he cannot hear *the* Voice. He is humanity in denial. Even though God shouts his holy love through nature, Scripture, and the manger, humans have pushed the mute button.

1. Bill Watterson, *Calvin and Hobbes*, December 21, 1987.

Later we will further explore how God speaks, when he speaks, to whom he speaks, and what he speaks—but for now it is enough to notice *that* he speaks. When it comes to communication, God started it. As Francis Schaffer says, "He is there, and he is not silent."[2] In nature, in Scripture, in Jesus, and through the ministry of the Holy Spirit, we hear the voice of God. In fact, not only does God speak, but he never stops talking.

If we open our mouths to speak, we reflect the self-revealing nature of God. If we open our ears to hear, we reflect his love. This is theology—truth about God—that makes a real-life difference when we are sipping coffee with a friend, negotiating business with a client, facing rebellion in a teen, or seeking peace across a color, culture, or class divide.

TRUTH TWO: HUMANS HAVE VALUE

Some Christmas ornaments—like those shiny ball ornaments that are boxed in twelves at the dollar store—are added to the tree simply in order to fill space and reflect lights. If they break, nobody sheds a tear. But other ornaments can be neither priced nor replaced. My most valued ornament is a little bird cut from yellow construction paper, which is hung on the tree with a piece of red yarn. Gayline, my bride of more than forty years, made it when she was eight—and it has been around ever since. I assure you that I give this ornament special care because of the one who made it. I do not touch it, handle it, or put it away except with gentle affection and tender respect. It gets treated extra well because it has extra value.

As it is with ornaments, so it is with humans. How *much* we value people determines how *well* we treat them. One key to just and merciful communication is to know others' true

2. See Francis A. Schaeffer, *He Is There and He Is Not Silent*, 30th anniv. ed. (Carol Stream, IL: Tyndale House, 2001).

value—which makes a biblical understanding of what it means to be human pretty important indeed.

The Christian gospel begins with the glorious news that *before* we became sinners in Adam, we were created as living icons of God.[3] We were made in God's image, as God's representative rulers and vice-regents on earth, to reflect his sovereign rule and holy love in this world (see Gen. 1:27–28). Yes, humans are now sinners who desperately need forgiveness. We need to be redeemed, regenerated, reclaimed, and restored if we are ever going to become all that we were meant to be. But depravity and dignity can coexist. Salvation doesn't bestow human glory; it restores it. God is redeeming believing sinners to enjoy the fully manifested glory in and for which all of us were made in the first place. He made us a little lower than the angels and crowned us with glory and honor (see Ps. 8:5), and through Jesus he is leading us into a glory that will surpass that of the angels (see Heb. 2:5–10).

This image—however defaced and disfigured by sin it may be now—is still there, even in the "worst" of us. *After* the Genesis 3 fall into sin, God says that every human is sacred still, because he or she is made in his image (see Gen. 9:6). Paul calls even the idolatrous Athenian pagans the *offspring of God*—a wondrous phrase that sets them (and all the rest of us) apart from all other creatures (see Acts 17:28–29). James says that when we curse another human we are cursing one who is made in the likeness of God (see James 3:9). Even in our vilest state, each of us still bears the image.

3. Thanks in part to the misguided science of recent times, this is a glory that has been lost and a dignity that is little felt by our neighbors, friends, and foes. This bequeaths to us a world without a creator God—and, if a world without a creator God, then a world without those who are created *in his image*. No God to know and love, and no image of God in which to discover true value. This is not only a denial of the truth but also a lousy deal.

The biblical doctrine of human value restores the glory of all of us—and also positions believers in particular to infuse a merciful, just, respectful, and loving quality into all our relationships before (and with) a watching world. Because we know that we are all made in the image, we know that there are no superiors or inferiors in the human family. No lessers or greaters. No lowers or highers. Just equals.

C. S. Lewis understood the implications of this, and he expressed them powerfully in these well-known words:

> The dullest and most uninteresting person you can talk to may one day be a creature which, if you saw it now, you would be strongly tempted to worship, or else a horror and a corruption such as you now meet, if at all, only in a nightmare. . . . It is in the light of these overwhelming possibilities, it is with the awe and the circumspection proper to them, that we should conduct all our dealings with one another, all friendships, all loves, all play, all politics. There are no *ordinary* people. You have never talked to a mere mortal. . . . It is immortals whom we joke with, work with, marry, snub, and exploit—immortal horrors or everlasting splendours.[4]

No doubt if you were to see me right now, you would question the *everlasting splendor* part of Lewis's words. At this very moment, my 6-foot, 4-inch, 240-pound hulk is slouched in my easy chair in post-dinner sloth—full, fat, frumpy, fallible, and fallen. And I mean *slouched*. To paraphrase Wodehouse, it looks like someone poured me into this chair and the chair forgot to say "When."[5] See me now and you would laugh at the incongruity between my present position and my future final condition. But

4. C. S. Lewis, *The Weight of Glory: And Other Addresses* (1949; repr., New York: Harper One, 2001), 45–46.

5. P. G. Wodehouse, *Very Good, Jeeves!* (1930; repr., New York: The Overlook Press, 2005), 33.

the Day is coming—and it is coming for all who believe—when the chair will be traded in for a throne. And on that Day I will slouch no more.

We are immortals traveling through life with immortals, eternal splendors conversing with eternal splendors, godlike beings interacting with godlike beings. This has major implications that inform what we are, what we're like, and how we're supposed to communicate. If we are godlike beings, then we should communicate like God does—and a commitment to doing so will dramatically and permanently alter our relationships with one another.

> Since it's God's image we reflect,
> Let us converse with deep respect.

TRUTH THREE: THE GOSPEL MATTERS

There is a glory in and about every human being—but you wouldn't be able to tell by the way we talk, and perhaps even less by how we listen. Too often our words sound like we're conversing with worms and weasels instead of wonders. Let's face it: we're wretched at this. James 3:9 stands like a condemning judge over our lives, and so does Matthew 12. Having told us, in verse 34 of that chapter, that our words are often careless because our *hearts* often couldn't care less, Jesus proceeds to say,

> I tell you, on the day of judgment people will give account for every careless word they speak, for by your words you will be justified, and by your words you will be condemned. (vv. 36–37)

His warning sets off a tremor in the soul. After all, who can count the careless words he or she has spoken?

Isaiah felt something more than a tremor in the temple one day. While worshiping, he saw the Lord seated on a throne. As the seraphs provided the soundtrack "Holy, holy, holy is the LORD of hosts," the holy glory of God filled the temple with smoke and the temple foundations shook. This temple quake produced aftershocks in Isaiah's soul, filling him with holy, humbled terror. He felt doom coming upon him as the blazing fire of God's holiness burned into his sinful heart. But as the piercing light penetrated Isaiah's darkness, perhaps to his surprise and to ours, what it revealed was not his immoral deeds or sinful actions or impure thoughts or unloving behavior, but his dirty mouth. "Woe is me!" he wailed. "For I am lost; for I am a man of unclean lips" (see Isa. 6:1–5).

When confronted with the holiness of God, Isaiah felt communication guilt and shame. He thought about all the bad things he had ever *said* more than about all the bad things he had ever done. The prophet whose calling was to speak the holy words of God felt doomed by all his own unholy words.

Thankfully, there's more to the Isaiah story. God cleansed Isaiah's lips with the touch of a coal from the sacrificial altar (Isa. 6:6–7). He assured Isaiah that forgiveness through sacrifice is real—yes, even for all the petty, nasty, and dirty things he had ever said. You and I need that gospel assurance as well—given how petty, nasty, and dirty our own mouths have been. We need to know that our sinful words have been atoned for through Jesus's guilt-removing, justice-satisfying, and wrath-appeasing death on the cross. We need a coal of divine mercy from the altar of Calvary to be placed upon our lips.

And we need Jesus's righteousness—his perfect words as well as his perfect deeds—to cover us before the throne of heaven. The obedient words and deeds of Jesus are a whiter-than-snow robe that covers our many sins, making us accepted and approved in the sight of God. This is, in part, what it means to be *in* or *in union with* Christ. Ephesians 1 and 2 teach us that in Christ we are chosen, redeemed, forgiven, adopted, lavishly graced, and, yes, destined for an eternal inheritance—despite the fact that we were born dead in sin (see Eph. 1:3–14; 2:1–3). This is true of every person who has ever turned in true faith to Christ. We are not just saved by Christ's atoning death; we are saved by his perfect words—which means that we can approach our speech problems from a place of gospel security before God.

STAYING TETHERED

Knowing that God speaks affects how we think about communication. Knowing that humans are made in the image affects how we think about those with whom we communicate. Knowing that we are washed in the blood and that we wear the robe affects how we think about all the communication messes we have made. As we stay tethered to these truths, let us now move on to biblical principle and practice.

Let's start fixing some pipes.

DISCUSSION AND REFLECTION

1. Consider the fact that God speaks, as well as the ways this chapter suggests that he does so. In what ways does he speak, and how do you take regular time to listen to him?
2. How do you know that God values you and others? What truths from the Bible confirm that he does?
3. "Since it's God's image we reflect, let us converse with deep respect" provides a starting point for communication. How does the truth that even your worst enemy is made in the image affect your thoughts about him or her?
4. Ephesians 1–3 present much of what it means to be "in Christ." From those chapters, create a list of all the spiritual blessings that the believer has through union with Jesus.
5. How can your union with Christ affect your relationships with others?

CHILL

OPEN UP

MAKE TIME

MEAN WHAT YOU SAY

UNDERSTAND WHAT YOU HEAR

NOURISH WITH GRACE

INITIATE PEACE

CELEBRATE OTHERS

ASSUME YOU ARE WRONG

THINK THE BEST

EXAMINE YOUR HEART

1

CHILL

"A soft answer turns away wrath, but a harsh word stirs up anger." (Prov. 15:1)

"Whoever restrains his words has knowledge, and he who has a cool spirit is a man of understanding." (Prov. 17:27)

To keep from war while in a spat,
Turn down your anger thermostat.

I had to learn early that it is not a good idea to rage and scream at immortals. Forty-five years ago, I was a mid-teen who was going places. People pegged me for a leader type. I was athletic enough to be a three-year, two-letter varsity sports jock, did the honor roll thing, attended church youth group, managed to have a friend or two, and even had a couple of girls who liked me (it helped that they wore very thick glasses). So you can imagine my surprise when a high school buddy named Bill told me that no one in my church youth group liked being around me—adding, with more than a little scorn, "Tim, you are so angry so often that everyone wants to stay away." Apparently there was something about my critical spirit and yelling tone that people didn't like. Go figure.

There was a history behind this. Check my bio and you'll see that I had a problem. Maybe I was so angry because I didn't feel like an immortal myself. After all, the young teen version of me had a zit problem that could have served in a pizza ad—or at least I assume so, since "Pizza Face" was the moniker that school bullies attached to me.

No doubt being the third of four highly competitive brothers didn't help, either. We were four apples that hadn't fallen far from a very competitive tree. None of us liked losing—but I was the worst. Defeat unleashed explosive words and destructive acts. My high school tennis coach could testify to this, since he had to replace several rackets that I smashed in my rage.

My brothers could confirm this, too—both the one over whose head I obliterated a ping-pong paddle and the one whose backside I smote with a two-by-four. For the record, I did *not* know there was a nail in that board. Only when he yelled as if Robin Hood had shot him did I realize that my assault had produced sharp-force as well as blunt-force trauma.

Despite all this, I was clueless about my problem until Bill's truth arrow pierced me through. In that moment, I knew that something was terribly wrong. Lifestyle choices and communication techniques had made me toxic, and I needed to change.

I tossed in bed that night with Bill's rebuke haunting my heart. "This is not how I want to do my life and relate to people," I thought. "This has to change. Yes, Lord, please help me to change. I must learn self-control." Right there, right then, empowered by grace, I made that choice. And change happened.

I tell this story because plenty of you can relate—and because I want you to have hope. Change can happen. I am sixty now and am awed by the power that Bill's words, through their anointing by the Spirit, released in me. His wounding words were my cure. I am amazed by it. God used Bill's rebuke to alter the course of anger in my life. In the forty-five years since, I've rarely yelled at anyone or had any kind of volatile outburst. Not that I've *never* expressed anger wrongly or hurt others in sinfully creative ways. I have—and way too many times. But I've been mostly cured of the sin of explosiveness, of temper tantrums, of angry outbursts and eruptions. And I'm pretty sure that all the image-bearers in my life are the happier for it.

Simply put—thanks to Bill, I learned to chill.

THE NEED TO CHILL

Given what we learned in the introduction to this book,[1] it is best not to holler and scream at future eternal splendors. Humans are worthy of better. Besides, because they are usually not fully aware of their own image-of-God status, they are likely to holler back.

The Proverbs of King Solomon tell us that we need to chill. With relentless repetition, Solomon insists that we rein in our emotions and calm down before we speak. How do you turn away someone's wrath? Give them a soft answer (see Prov. 15:1). How do you quiet contention? Don't be hot tempered, and do be slow to anger (see Prov. 15:18). How do you stop a quarrel-flood from pouring out? Have a cool spirit, and quit the argument before it even starts (see Prov. 17:14, 27). Do you want to keep anger from igniting? Remove the kindling of a quarrelsome spirit (see Prov. 26:21). What happens when you give full vent to your spirit? You only prove yourself a fool (see Prov. 29:11). And what if you choose to be full of wrath and given to anger? All that you will get out of it is a lot of strife and sin (see Prov. 29:22).

These ancient sayings contrast the effects of a quiet response with those of a noisy one. A failure to chill fuels the flames of conflict, while a decision to chill douses the fire. In a conflict, anger tends to be parasitic; it finds a host organism—usually the other

1. I recommend that if you did not read this book's introduction, you go back and do so. It is a helpful foundation for all that follows.

person's anger—and sucks its virulent life from it. Anger begets anger, and intense heat causes intense quarrels. Somebody has to chill, or it's going to get ugly.

If coolness of spirit ends strife, then at times a good stiff conversation with self is in order. We must secure a tight, two-fisted grab on our own collars and, with a full eyeball-to-eyeball gaze into our own inner being, say, "Self. Get a grip. Chill. Calm down. Compose thyself." We need to speak with authority and then listen up. If we don't, what might have started as merely a little tiff will likely turn into war.

> To keep from war while in a spat,
> Turn down your anger thermostat.

FROM PROVERBS TO IMPERATIVES

For Paul, this is serious truth. Ancient proverb becomes binding imperative in Ephesians 4:31: "Let all bitterness and wrath and anger and clamor and slander be put away from you, along with all malice." With full apostolic authority, Paul forbids several hotheaded sins in one rapid-fire sequence.

- *Bitterness* is very angry hurt or offense that poisons a relationship. It is when my offense over your actions or words sours my thoughts about you and poisons my ability to love you with a sincere and affectionate heart.
- *Wrath* is passionate anger that produces attitudes, words, and actions that are generated and fueled by emotions.
- *Anger* is wrath in action—acted-out wrath.
- *Clamor* refers to angry outbursts. It is high-decibel anger: voice-raising, door-slamming, table-pounding, wall-punching fury.[2]

2. Paul makes it clear that while it may not always be wrong to be angry (see

- *Slander* is unnecessary negative speech about another person. It's anytime I speak of somebody's real or imagined badness, unless it is absolutely needed for the good of someone involved.
- *Malice* is evil intention or ill will. It is when the heart goes dark. The light of kindness, goodness, and grace is snuffed out, and the only thing that remains is the will to hurt, harass, and harm people who are made in the image of God.

All of these are hotheaded sins—vices that explode with deadly effect upon the scene of our relationships. And Paul says that we need to let *all* of *all* of them be put away from us. "Get rid of it all," he warns, adding in another place that those who make a habit of "enmity, strife . . . [and] fits of anger . . . will not inherit the kingdom of God" (Gal. 5:20–21). This is serious. You cannot be right with God and be habitually trashing those who are made in his image.

While Paul tells us what *not* to do in anger, James tells us what *should* be done in love. Paul commands us to take off the old clothes of raging sin, and James tells us to put on a new wardrobe of heavenly grace. We need to pray for wisdom, he says (see James 1:5–7)—and such wisdom, which is from above, is "first pure, then peaceable, gentle, open to reason, full of mercy and good fruits, impartial and sincere" (James 3:17). *Gentle* is the key word here. The Greek word behind it carries the meaning of being measured, mild, and moderate in our responses to others—the opposite of belligerent, argumentative, and quarrelsome. A calm and tranquil heart defuses angry conflict simply by refusing to enter it.

On occasion, some will be infuriated when a gentle person

Eph. 4:26), it is almost always wrong to make a lot of noise when we are. Loud anger is not a personality or cultural thing; it is a sin thing—and Paul tells us to be done with it.

refuses to share their fury. I've witnessed people rage against others for not raging back, because they wanted either some justification to keep raging or the satisfaction of pushing another person over the edge. But such are the exceptions. As a rule, a soft answer turns away wrath. And even if it does not, it is still the right path to take.

CHILLING IS A CHOICE

You may assume that you're not wired to chill. It's not who you are, and it's not possible for it ever to be. Some are peaceful types, while others are not so much. And you're convinced that you are among the not-so-much crowd. But don't despair. There. Is. Hope.

How long do you think you can go without losing your temper? Stop and think before you answer. The world has the flat-out wrong answer on this one, my friend. From Sesame Street days on up, a culture that is committed to unrestrained self-expression has programmed millions not to hold back when having an anger attack. I remember the scenes—and I'm guessing they're still standard fare on that venerable kids' show—when grownups extolled the virtues of venting to Cookie Monster, Bert, and Ernie. Let it out. Holler loud. Punch a pillow. Slam a door. Speak your mind. Be real. It's not healthy to hold it in. There are times when you've got to spew.

The mantras of self-expression, and the supposed perils of suppressed anger, have been repeated so long and so often that they have taken on "Thou shalt" and "Thou shalt not" status for many. A generation has been bred to think that speaking your mind is more honorable than taming your tongue—that the greatest virtue is to let it all out via talk, tweet, text, or tirade. What does it matter if you're not sure it's true, or if there isn't any real need to say it? What does it matter if reputations are ruined and lives are destroyed? Nowadays, it seems that people are guilty of anger mismanagement only if they *fail* to release the fury of accusing wrath. When we heat up and explode, leaving a host of temper-traumatized victims in our wake, we claim innocence: "I couldn't help it. I had to speak my mind. I had to be real. I believe in calling it like I see it." Funny how it's always someone else's issues we're seeing.

Let me ask the question again: How long can we go without losing it? A day? Two days? A week? Anyone for a month? The answer is simply this: *we can go as long as we choose.* Chilling is a choice. In every conflict, we have at least a fleeting awareness when a moment of decision arrives. "I shouldn't say this, but . . ." "I know that this isn't right or fair, but . . ." "This is wrong, but . . ." "I shouldn't be yelling, but . . ." Every conflict has a hinge point of hesitation—a full or split second when we pause at the decision intersection and *choose.*

FROM HYSTERICS TO CALM

Back in the day, we had a volatile older couple who hovered on the fringes of our church. To say that Bert and Harriet had anger issues is like saying that Pompeii might want to keep an eye on Vesuvius, with each alternating as Vesuvius on any given day. I tried often to help them, but it was slow going. Compounding the problem was that they were in their seventies while I was still around forty. It's always awkward to do intensive marriage counseling for people who are more than old enough to be your parents.

One evening, my post-dinner quiet was interrupted by a panicked call from Bert pleading for my help. It was a "clergy 911"—the kind that every pastor dreads. While it's a privilege to serve in life's war zones, it's no fun to be called into a family crisis that's been brewing for decades and to be expected somehow to fix it in minutes.

Over the phone, I could hear Harriet in the background, screaming hysterically. Her uncontrolled rage gushed with a torrential force that required intervention. As I drove to their home, I prayed for help—and made sure to have a phone handy to call the other 911. Given her past psychological issues, I was pretty sure that Harriet would need to be restrained and hospitalized. That I found her crouching behind some large plants in her living room, still in raging hysterics, confirmed the worst of my fears.

As I observed Harriet's ongoing and escalating rage, an idea that was born of desperation came to my mind. It might work, given that I'd built up some relational equity with Harriet. I was semi-sure that she trusted me. So, quietly and slowly, I walked up to Harriet, put my hands gently on both her shoulders, looked her squarely in the eyes, and said with a gentle but *very* firm voice, "Harriet. Be *quiet*." It was the verbal equivalent of a lifeguard slapping a struggling swimmer whose panic has overcome her sense.

Harriet's eyes changed instantly. Their wild rage and fear gave way to calm. Within seconds, her hysterics stopped and her spirit quieted; she came out from behind the bushes and sat down beside me to begin a normal conversation. Two hours of relentless and unbridled rage had ended in mere moments. It was a matter of choice, as it almost always is.

Chapter 11 will show that what controls our hearts determines our emotions, words, and behavior. We will see that, just like Harriet, all of us who seem to be out of control and to have no power over our emotions can gain sudden self-control when a new desire tips the scales of our motivation in favor of self-restraint.

This is a key first step in communication. Self-control is a Holy Spirit–given ability (see Gal. 5:22–23) to restrain emotions, words, and actions and stay peacefully calm even when a storm hits. If you are a Christian, you have the power to say no to volatile, sinfully expressed anger. There isn't any temptation we face that we can't escape (see 1 Cor. 10:13). God's promises are all that we need for life and godliness (see 2 Peter 1:3–4). The grace that has saved us also teaches us to live self-controlled lives in which we renounce sinful ways by speaking a firm, committed, decisive, and life-altering no to what is wrong (see Titus 2:11–12). God is at work in us to enable us both to "will and to work for his good pleasure" (Phil. 2:13). He gives what it takes in order to chill.

BUT WHY IS CHILLING SO HARD?

But if it is true that God enables us to control our sinful choices, then why is chilling so hard? Why is it so much easier to speak of self-control than it is to exercise it—as our universally shared life experience clearly proves? "No human being can tame the tongue," James asserts—and he has good reason to say so. Explosive anger is so commonplace and feels so natural that it seems more like an unavoidable human frailty than a matter of deliberate and correctible sin. But it is *both* weakness, which requires divine enablement, and wickedness, which requires personal attention and intentional action.

It is helpful to start recognizing the factors that catalyze our angry emotion. These do not *cause* our angry emotion—for nothing causes our angry reactions except the ruling desires and cravings of our own hearts (see James 4:1–2). But they do affect us and set us off. As we learn from various Bible characters, there are countless triggers that must be recognized and countered in our lives.

Angry Person(s)	Anger Trigger	Angry Act	Do They Chill?
Cain (Gen. 4:1–16)	rejection by God	murder	No. And God banishes him when he fails to repent.
Sarah (Gen. 21:8–10)	a bullied son	banishment of Ishmael and his mother	No. And millennia of strife ensue.

Angry Person(s)	Anger Trigger	Angry Act	Do They Chill?
Dinah's brothers (Gen. 34:5–30)	rape of their sister	trickery and violent vengeance	No. And they bring trouble for the family.
Joseph's brothers (Gen. 37:5–8, 18–28)	sibling rivalry	selling their brother into slavery and lying to their father	Yes. But only after years of hardship and grief.
Moses (Num. 20:10–13)	whining followers	disobedience to God's command	Yes. But only after losing his entrance into the promised land.
Balaam (Num. 22:27–35)	a stubborn animal	beating his donkey	Yes. But only after he is confronted by an angel with a sword.
Saul (1 Sam. 18:6–11)	jealousy and insecurity	paranoia and attempted murder	No. And he and David continue to be at odds.
David (1 Sam. 25:1–13, 21–35)	injustice and ingratitude	planning a bloodbath	Yes. But only after Abigail confronts him.
Job (Job 23:1–7; 27:2; 40:2–8)	grief and suffering	questioning God	Yes. But only after divine correction.

Angry Person(s)	Anger Trigger	Angry Act	Do They Chill?
Nebuchadnezzar (Dan. 3:1–30)	a wounded ego	throwing three men into a fire	Yes. But only after divine intervention and power.
Jonah (Jonah 4:5–11)	removal of physical comfort	self-pity and a hardened heart	Unknown.
Caiaphas (Matt. 26:57–68)	unwanted truth	brutal injustice and torture	No. And he calls for Jesus's crucifixion.
James and John (Luke 9:51–55)	people's rejection of Jesus	asking if they can destroy the people with fire from heaven	Yes. But only after Jesus rebukes them.
Peter (John 18:10–11)	fear	cutting off a man's ear	Yes. But only after Jesus tells him to stop.
Paul (Acts 23:2–5)	physical assault	accidentally disrespecting a leader	Yes. But only after he realizes his error.

Did you notice that there are familiar biblical heroes among the number of those who lost it from time to time? Let that comfort you as you go to war with your anger. Even the best of saints has anger triggers. We all do. And it helps us to be alert to what they are. Take another look at the "Anger Trigger" column to see how varied triggers can be, and consider how familiar the ones here are to your own life. At least twelve of them map on to my own experience! Observe, too, that the anger catalysts are not always sinful in themselves, even though the angry acts are.

All of this is what makes chilling so hard. We lose our chill easily because we have so many emotional vulnerabilities and weak points—*and* because there are so many things that happen in this world that can legitimately make us angry, but which we nevertheless need to process with restraint. This is no easy task, but it is possible. Yet it will be possible only when we recognize the hair triggers that most often set off our own anger, become aware of when we are most vulnerable, and make sure that our trigger locks are in working order.

A GOD AND GOSPEL MOMENT

Another thing that helps our pursuit of self-control is an awareness of what God is like and of how we are to be like him. Paul reminds us of this in Colossians 3:8–10 when he teaches that hotheaded sins are not fitting for those of us who "have put on the new self, which is being renewed . . . after the image of its creator" (v. 10). When we fail to chill, we fail to be like God. We misrepresent the image in us when we attack the image in others.

Consider for a moment the One whose image we bear. *God is not hot-tempered*. He is patient and gentle with us every day. When we think about chilling, we are thinking about being like God—about treating others the way God treats us.

Way back in Exodus 33:18–19, Moses prayed, "Please show me your glory," to which God responded, "I will make all my goodness pass before you." Then,

> The Lord descended in the cloud and stood with him there, and proclaimed the name of the Lord. The Lord passed before him and proclaimed, 'The Lord, the Lord, a God merciful and gracious, slow to anger, and abounding in steadfast love and faithfulness, keeping steadfast love for thousands. (Ex. 34:5–7)

When God revealed his glorious goodness to Moses, what did he say? What is the blazing center of his manifest presence? God is *merciful and gracious, slow to anger*. The Hebrew term for *slow* simply means "long." You and I have to offend God many times, over a very long time, without any repentance, before his fuse burns down. His mercy and grace in the face of human sin are longsuffering. There is nothing of the impulsive, the reactionary, the rash, or the explosive about God.

Herein lies one facet of the glory of God. He is a patient and gentle God. His responses to our sins are never volatile. When he does get angry at human sin, it is always proportionate—in keeping with holiness, patience, and justice. Our text teaches us that it is the glory of God that he is long-fused and gentle in response to all our junk. Moses saw God's glory—even if but a fringe of it—and what he saw was that God is amazingly merciful and wonderfully slow to anger. And I am glad.

One of the great wonders of my life is that God hasn't squashed me today. Despite my many sins, he hasn't yelled and screamed, or pounded his fist, or slammed the door and walked away. Quite the opposite—he has poured out kindness upon kindness. And when he has confronted me, it hasn't been with severe word and stern face. It has been with a firm but ever-so-gentle whisper to my conscience, a quiet voice in my inner man, a wooing of my heart toward greater holiness, a renewed invitation to be like him.

This is God's way, and it is his glory. He is patient about our impatience, calm in the face of our clamor, quiet while correcting our quarreling. He holds his tongue and stills his emotions, even while we fail to do the same. When we chill, we mirror the heart of God. We offer to others what has been so gloriously given to us.

WHEN THE RINGTONE SOUNDS

Dinner is prepared. The table is set. The kids' hands are washed. Everything is nearly ready. But the bliss is interrupted when mischievous little Cadan does his milk version of a Gatorade victory celebration, thoroughly damping everything and dousing the meatloaf. After a momentary out-of-body experience in which you hover above your world gone awry, you look, as old Mr. Wodehouse would say, "like a tomato struggling for self-expression."[3] Cadan quickly rues his celebration—not because he's made a mess of dinner but because you, his parent, have suddenly transformed into a fire-breathing dragon.

You've got flaming eyes and steaming ears. As your lid flips, you find your tongue. Your volcanic rant spews on, blaming, shaming, and defaming in raw molten anger. And with each passing second, the little guy puddles further into fear and shame.

And then your church small group leader's (or, even worse, your *pastor's*) ringtone goes off on you. It's playing the new hit "I Need to Save Face," and suddenly it's decision time. You know how this plays out, right? Imagine Cadan's awe when before his wondering eyes you transform from dragon to lamb and, with an artificially sweetened tone, you pick up the phone and offer the nicest, kindest, gentlest, most welcoming "Hello" the world has ever heard.

Split-second self-control. Instant chill. It's enough to make you think, isn't it? Maybe we don't just *have* to let it out after all. When a temper tantrum can be stilled in a second, it proves at least one thing: chilling is a choice.

So the next time your button gets pushed, what will you choose? To be like God (see Eph. 4:31–5:2), or to play the fool (see Prov. 14:29)? To indulge angry passion, or to respect the image? God calls us to imitate him—to renounce angry outbursts, temper flare-ups, and volatile eruptions and to deplore them all for the sins that they are. Life with others calls for light without heat. Conversations go nowhere, and relationships don't get even that far, unless we chill.

3. P. G. Wodehouse, *Right Ho, Jeeves* (1934; repr., New York: W. W. Norton, 2011), 211.

So let's be like God, and, with the assurance that he will enable what he commands, let's put the lid on it and calm down.

DISCUSSION AND REFLECTION

1. How often do you lose your temper?
2. How does your anger normally manifest itself (for example, through yelling, moping, sulking, cursing, and so on)?
3. What are frequent triggers for your anger?
4. If "to keep from war while in a spat [you need to] turn down your anger thermostat," what might be some helpful steps you could take to lower your temperature before you speak?
5. Describe a time when you failed to chill. Was there a moment when you were conscious of making a choice in your anger—when you knew you should stop? How did you respond to it?

CHILL

OPEN UP

MAKE TIME

MEAN WHAT YOU SAY

UNDERSTAND WHAT YOU HEAR

NOURISH WITH GRACE

INITIATE PEACE

CELEBRATE OTHERS

ASSUME YOU ARE WRONG

THINK THE BEST

EXAMINE YOUR HEART

2

OPEN UP

"Let the redeemed of the Lord say so." (Ps. 107:2)

"If your brother sins against you,
go and tell him his fault, between you
and him alone." (Matt. 18:15)

"Better is open rebuke than hidden love.
Faithful are the wounds of a friend." (Prov. 27:5–6)

To keep your heart and spirit closed
Does far more harm than is supposed.

The situation was dire. Sam and Pam were in my office again, just as they had been many times before. Their marriage had been a domestic twelve-year war—an in-house (un)civil conflict of epic proportions. Open hostilities were the rule. Temporary cease-fires were the exception. Real peace seemed like a pipe dream. In their relationship, the active aggression was mostly her fault—*sort of*. His anger was a steaming pot; hers, a boiling and roiling Mount St. Helens. Yet neither of them could (or would) say where all the anger was coming from.

"BUT YOU NEVER TOLD ME!"

Pam knew how to be angry really well. She sustained a level of uninterrupted anger that was close to unrivaled in my counseling experience. Frankly, it was impressive. It takes a special determined effort to stay that mad for that long! Some of her anger was passive-aggressive, but most of it was just plain aggressive—an in-his-face anger, defiance, and antagonism that worked at cross-purposes to Sam at every opportunity.

I spent countless hours—probably too many—trying to help them to work through their issues, but with no progress to show for it. We were stuck. Having nothing more to say or to pray, I made a last-ditch effort to break through. Turning to Pam, I pleaded for cooperation: "Pam, can you think of something—even just one thing—that Sam did to you way back when, which is the root of all this anger? Is there anything that started this war?"

For some inexplicable reason, she chose this moment to reveal her heart. "Yes, there is something. Twelve years ago, Sam made me make a decision that I did not want to make. He decided that our family's future was going to go in a direction I did not want to go. And I have been angry ever since."

As Pam filled in the details, I searched Sam's nonverbals to gauge his reaction. His face wore an expression like that of someone who, expecting a report of a muscle strain, has just been told he has cancer. He was torn between disbelief and dismay.

When given a chance, he said simply, "Pam, I didn't know. You never told me that you disagreed with that decision—not then, and not since. This is the first time I've ever heard that you opposed it or that it had anything to do with our conflicts." It was true. By her own admission, Pam had held him hostage to her rage for twelve years without ever once telling him why.

I knew I had to look for the backstory. People don't usually commit this kind of relational hara-kiri without cause. After all, Pam really had loved Sam at one point—and still did, even if it was with all the warm expression of a frozen fish. There had to be history here. Nothing could excuse her sins, but something had to explain her anger. And there was something. When I wrote earlier that Pam and Sam's struggles were "mostly her fault—*sort of*," the *sort of* was a tractor-trailer-sized qualifier that carried the massive tonnage of blame belonging to Sam.

The fact is that Sam hadn't led his wife through that decision with much wisdom, humility, or love. He had failed to cherish her with the winsome grace that she needed in order to feel safe making open conversation and even contradicting him. He was an opinionated guy who bulldozed over others' input—including Pam's. He was not the kind of husband who infused a "Why, yes! Let's be open and honest!" freedom into his marriage. He was strong on answers, explanations, actions, and results while weaker on the nourishing and cherishing side of things. God alone knows, but I suspect that there was a whole lot of blame to go around.

Still, I couldn't help but mourn. If only Pam had somehow found a way to open up, and if only Sam had nurtured a relationship with her in which she felt safe to do so. Openness is the path to peace. If she had dared to be honest, she would never have become so angry. If, encouraged by him, she had spoken a few carefully expressed words of honest opinion and courageous contradiction in their hour of fateful decision, they both might well have been preserved from twelve years of fury.

Thankfully, Pam and Sam both trust the Savior and won't face eternal wrath for their prolonged marital Gettysburg. But oh! what tears will be shed on the final Day for the twelve years of wrath that they put each other through while on earth.

COMMUNICATION REQUIRES WORDS

If openness is the path to peace and joy, then why don't more people open up? The reasons are many and varied. Some people simply don't like to talk much. They are temperamentally reserved. Some guard against saying the wrong thing so carefully that they seldom say anything. Some don't want to sound argumentative or angry or offensive or just plain stupid. Some worry so much about what others think that they never say what they themselves think. Some choose to say nothing rather than to face the retaliation that they fear their honest words may ignite. Some create a chamber of prolonged silence in which to torture offenders or extract concessions from communication-deprived victims. Some think that the best way not to *blow* up (that is, the best way to *chill*) is simply to *clam* up. But the truth is that a choice not to speak—if sustained over time, for whatever reason—is a choice not to love.

Body language and nonverbal communication matter, but communication requires words if it is to bind hearts together as one. Anger never dissipates, wounds never heal, understanding never happens, the marital two-into-one process that God initiates never deepens, loneliness never gives way to friendship, and the racial, class, and political divides never close, unless people open up and talk. Silence leads to distance, to ignorance, to indifference, to intolerance—all of which in turn lead to defiance, abhorrence, and belligerence. In order for us to break that vicious cycle, what's inside us has to come out.

> To keep your heart and spirit closed
> Does far more harm than is supposed.

OH, SAY WHAT YOU SEE

The Scriptures call us to open honesty—to *say what we see.* Our Lord himself commands it: "If your brother sins against you, go and tell him his fault, between you and him alone. If he listens to you, you have gained your brother" (Matt. 18:15). The apostle Paul pleads with us to do it: "[Be] speaking the truth in love"[1] (Eph. 4:15). Old Solomon advises it: "Better is open rebuke than hidden love. Faithful are the wounds of a friend" (Prov. 27:5–6). And again our Lord models it:

> You are my friends if you do what I command you. No longer do I call you servants, for the servant does not know what his master is doing; but I have called you friends, for *all that I have heard from my Father I have made known to you.* (John 15:14–15)

Prophet, apostle, and Savior alike all call us to turn our words into windows so that others can see into our minds and hearts.

We get a fuller picture of what this looks like when James concludes his hard-hitting call for us to have a bridled tongue and a holy life with a series of commands for us to *open up*.

> Is anyone among you suffering? Let him pray. Is anyone cheerful? Let him sing praise. Is anyone among you sick? Let him call for the elders of the church, and let them pray over him. . . . Therefore, confess your sins to one another and pray for one another, that you may be healed. . . .
>
> My brothers, if anyone among you wanders from the truth and someone brings him back, let him know that whoever brings back a sinner from his wandering will save his soul from death and will cover a multitude of sins. (James 5:13–14, 16, 19–20)

According to James, if you're a healthy Christian, you won't internalize. If you are suffering, you will talk to God about it in prayer. If you are cheerful, you'll vocalize it in song. If you are sick, you won't keep it a secret but will talk to your pastor-elders about it so that they in turn can talk to God about it through intercession. If you are in a sin pattern, you won't hide. Rather, you will talk with

1. Contextually, Paul means both objective doctrinal truth and simple, honest truth-telling.

others about it through confession. And if you see fellow believers wandering off the path, you won't simply wish that they were in a better place. You will go after them and talk to them so that you can restore them. After all, you cannot bring a sinner back from his wandering unless you talk to him about his wandering.

In all these ways and more, we should be *saying* what we are *seeing*—whether we're seeing it in the mirror or in our neighbor. We need to be open and honest—just like God is.

PRACTICING THE IMAGE

God is a talking God. He opens up, relating to us through words as he discloses his heart, his aims, his desires, his sorrows, his plans, his love. We need not wander aimlessly in the dark or guess what God thinks of us or wants from us or expects of us or promises to us.

But God's openness is not only a source of direction and comfort for us. It is also a model for us to imitate. It is a part of God-*like*-ness—an aspect of being made in the image of God—that we can talk. It is a part of god-*li*-ness that we open up and disclose ourselves to others. Our capacity to open lines of communication in order to transfer thoughts, dreams, concerns, and knowledge from our hearts to others lays the foundation for what is the essence of relationship and love. It's a way for us to take part in the loving communication that flows forth from the very nature of God.

What Tony Evans says of the racial divide in the church applies to all of our divisions and relationship challenges: "It takes more than a hug or a friendly 'hello' to bridge the gap."[2] It takes work—a committed effort that goes far beyond a glib "Hello"—to achieve true knowledge and understanding of others. We have to make the "necessary effort to get to know each other on a level

2. Tony Evans, *Oneness Embraced: Through the Eyes of Tony Evans* (Chicago: Moody Publishers, 2011), 31.

of an authentic exchange. Without a basis of shared knowledge, purposes, and mutual respect, we cannot come together for any meaningful impact."[3] We would do well to take that advice and apply it to every important relationship in our lives.

Such transparent openness is best done in person. Face to face is better than all other options—though other options have their value. Technology is cool, to be sure. In between these paragraphs, I'm checking ESPN for updates about my Red Sox's latest beatdown of the Yankees. My phone just beeped with the news that my twelfth grandchild is being delivered a hundred miles away. And now a return text is leaping from my phone to my son's, sharing the joy of the arrival of his first son. Even this simple dabbling in high-tech communication amazes me.

But this is nothing compared to what can happen in face-to-face relationship. A smiling emoji will soon be replaced with some other trendy graphic. But a smiling *face* is irreplaceable. A handshake, a pat on the back, and a hug to say "Well done" will never be improved. A clicked "Like" button says something. But a smile, a nod, and a word that says "That's really cool" (or *wonderful* or *good*) says a whole lot more. A meme that is posted for whoever happens to see it is the latest rage. But a *me* who enters your world with words, spirit, and heart leads to lasting love. All this is what it means to bear the image.

SO WHAT SHALL WE TALK ABOUT?

To be clear, opening up does not mean opening fire. But it means realizing that the fix for blowing up is not clamming up. To be chill is not to passively tolerate wrongdoing or wrong thinking. Rather, as those who bear the image, we can enter into relationships with others with a courageous commitment to speak ourselves, with love, into their lives.

3. Evans, 31.

In case you are out of practice, let me offer a crash course on the content of such a courageous, committed conversation you might have with someone. "What would we talk about?" might be the question on many minds. The answer depends on where you are in your relationship with each person you are communicating with and on how deeply you trust and feel safe with that person. Once it is tailored to the context of the relationship, a conversation can go in many different directions. Here are some ideas.

Talk about God's redeeming and transforming grace. If God has been good to you, talk about it. Tell your redemption story—both its past and its present. Share the wonders of what he has done. "Let the redeemed of the LORD say so" (Ps. 107:2).

Talk about what you like. I like peanut butter. I could eat thick and juicy peanut butter and jelly sandwiches for lunch, every day, without a whisper of discontent. I like peanut butter ice cream, peanut butter cups, peanut butter squares, peanut butter plain. Give it to me in layers, give it to me by the spoonful, give it to me on a shovel. That's why it's so crazy that not until thirty-seven years into our married life did Gayline realize that my peanut butter of choice was Jif. I'm not sure why I never told the primary shopper in our family what I *liked.* I just didn't—which meant that for thirty-seven years I was eating second-rate peanut butter and jelly sandwiches when I could have had better. Don't do that, folks—talk about what you like. Start with peanut butter. Then proceed from there.

Talk about what you appreciate. I'll devote a whole chapter to the ministry of encouraging and celebrating others later on in this book, but for now, realize this: relationships grow deep and strong when we take the time to share what we appreciate about others, about God, and about life.

Talk about what God is teaching you. Share with others what you are learning from God's Word, or through suffering, or from fellowship and preaching, or from a good book.

Talk about what gives you joy. Talk about what makes you happy, what makes you smile, what fills you with delight.

Talk about what makes you sad. Do not hide your tears from others. It's impossible to weep with those who weep (see Rom. 12:15) if all of us shed our tears only in private.

Talk about what you fear. All of us are afraid of something. Me? I'm afraid of failure. Others are afraid of oppression, being alone, job loss, actual physical harm, abuse. Some are afraid of racism, while others are afraid of being called racist because of something they've said. Some fear the ongoing effects of sexism, while others fear inadvertently contributing to the gender war. When we share our fears and our tears, we deepen understanding, affection, and solidarity and invite others into our struggles.

Talk about what you're doing wrong. James teaches us to confess our sins to one another. We do well to walk in the light rather than in the night. Life in the shadows is life in danger. Transparency leads to brother-and-sister-in-arms comradery, as well as to spiritual freedom and transformation.

Talk about what offends you. If you're offended by someone's serious or repeated or reckless or dangerous sins, Jesus says to speak up (see Matt. 18:15). And whatever you do, don't play the "If he doesn't know what he did wrong, I'm not telling him" card. If someone offends you, let him or her know with humble but courageous grace. And if people ask you what they've done wrong, oblige them with an honest answer—not in order to condemn or punish but in order to heal and restore, as Jesus also says. Remember my teenaged friend Billy's rebuke. It changed my life. Who knows what type of monster I'd be today if he hadn't opened up?

Talk about what others need to hear. Seek and find and bring back wanderers. Admonish, warn, and exhort them (Heb. 3:12–13; James 5:19–20).

Talk about what you suspect. In Joshua 22:10–31, the tribes of Israel were on the brink of war with one another (see v. 12) because of suspicion. They would have gone to war over a misunderstanding—if they hadn't at the last minute talked about what ten of the tribes suspected the other two of doing. It's a good thing that someone thought to ask before they began to act.

I read somewhere of a marriage that was in crisis for reasons that were unknown to the husband, until one day his wife finally opened up in counseling and accused him of cheating on her. When the counselor asked why she thought so, she traced her suspicions to missing money: her husband had left a decent amount unaccounted for. At that point the husband drew out his wallet and removed all the "missing" money. His explanation? He had been saving it up for their wedding anniversary!

By not opening up, she allowed her fears and suspicions to fester over time, until they led her all the way to a counselor's office—and all for nothing. Suspicion that is unaddressed leads to mutual distrust. It also can rob people of the very accountability they need in order to stop doing, or to keep from doing, the very things that are suspected of them. It may be that what you suspect is true, and that the suspect needs to know that he or she is not getting away with it, in order to come clean.[4]

4. Caution: be careful with suspicion. You don't want to become a suspicious or cynical person (as we will see in chapter 10). And you *do* want to make sure that you express suspicion as perception, not as accusation. Be humble—your suspicion may be wrong. Still, when there is reason for concern—especially if

Talk about what you need. I think of a friendship of mine—one that started as more of a counselor-to-counselee relationship. At one point I ended an email to this brother-counselee by saying, "BTW—would you please pray for me? My headache has been acting up a bit, and I need grace." His response: "Tim, I am praying for you. And Tim—thanks for inviting me to care for you like that!" Our relationship took a positive turn from there.

Talk about your aspirations and plans. As Jesus did when he told his friends what he and the Father were aiming to do (see John 15:15), let's share our plans and invite others into them. Dreaming out loud about aspirations and goals welcomes the input and excitement of others.

Talk about what has been done to you. In a very serious vein, there is another kind of opening up that may well be life-and-death. Survivors of abuse or other grievous sins or violent acts need to find safe people with whom to share. Because I believe this issue is far more serious and widespread than most of us dare to think, I believe that it needs to be addressed. This sensitive topic needs careful nuance and compassionate response. But it is important that survivors of abuse have safe places to go where they can find refuge and seek justice—and I would encourage each to seek them out.

Talk about what you disagree with. This can be one of the harder applications of the "open up" principle—not because disagreeing is hard, but because disagreeing in a godly way is. We humans disagree very well. But disagreeing in an open and constructive way, especially over important matters, requires supernatural courage and humility—and may also require a little extra advice.

---

suspicion produces distrust in your relationships or might leave the suspect in spiritual peril if he is not warned—express your humble concern.

I've often thought about how much better things would have gone if Sapphira had disagreed with Ananias and interrupted his scheming plans (see Acts 5:1–11). It would surely have helped if she had interjected, "Hey, Ananias, dear, do you really think this is going to work? Lying to God doesn't seem like such a good idea. I'm not so sure we can fool the Holy Spirit—or that Jesus will be too happy if we try." Her open disagreement would have helped. But she didn't disagree openly—and, if normal human experience is any indicator, the reason may have been because she and Ananias never learned how to do it well.

Constructive disagreement may require that we find a safe context where we can discover common ground, practice good listening, seek understanding, and learn and grow together. Safe contexts may include a public space where volume will stay low, or a third party who can mediate and urge caution, or agreed-on rules of engagement for processing the disagreement.

DISAGREEMENT: BRIDGING THE GAPS BETWEEN US

Disagreements can be hard, but God gives us the grace to work through them if we resolve to process them with love. Here are several suggestions for easing the way forward.

- *Pray for grace to help.* Disagreeing in a godly way requires God's grace.
- *Prepare notes / main points.* It helps us to think beforehand about what is most important to say and how best to say it.
- *Meet in a public or safe place.* In order to guard against communicating sinfully during strong

disagreements, it might be wise for us to avoid conversations behind closed doors or without a referee.

- *Find common ground.* We are more inclined to listen with respect when we start with points of agreement and mutual understanding.
- *Practice COMMUNICATE.* A biblical communication lifestyle is the best way to process disagreement.
- *Don't seek light while feeling the heat.* If we have not chosen to chill before having our disagreements, heated exchanges will be far more likely, and we will be far less likely to see the light of truth.
- *Express perceptions—not assertions.* Since disagreements are often caused by misunderstandings, we do well to start with what we think we see rather than with what we're "sure" we know.
- *Don't dump; unload.* It is better for us to unload our concerns one piece at a time than to back up the truck and dump a full load of gripes on others.
- *Consider mediation.* If one-on-one resolution doesn't happen, agree to get some outside help.
- *Seek progress—not perfection.* Consider that taking a few steps forward is better than standing still or going backward.
- *Anticipate learning.* As we will see in chapter 9, it's very likely that we are at least partly wrong, so we do well to anticipate that we will learn from our disagreements.
- *Await heaven for closure.* Since only heaven will make everything right, we must be content with the incomplete for now.

YOU'VE GOTTA START SOMEWHERE

Opening up is a lifelong process in which we share whatever is appropriate for any given relationship—and it's a process that needs a push. When I went to a Bible college to pursue pastoral ministry, I had two major people problems. First, I dreaded speaking *in front of* people (how I hated speech class!). Second, I equally disliked speaking *to* people. Up until my early twenties, I was shy enough (or selfish enough) to avoid talking to people whenever possible—which included redirecting my route down a different church aisle if I saw people approaching. And when people knocked, I'd let Gayline answer the door while I snuck off to the other end of the house.

The more I've thought about this, the more ashamed I am. I am sure now that my hatred of speech class was a double fear (first of man and then of failure), while my avoidance of conversation was nothing less than a simple, selfish lack of love. I preferred my own little uninterrupted world and was quite content there. I wasn't into relationships. Listening, caring, and being vulnerable, connected, and helpful were too much work. And all the while, I wanted to be a pastor!

I have never forgotten the time that the Spirit awakened me to myself through this question: "Tim, how can you claim to love people and want to serve the church if in fact you are not even willing to talk to people?"

Since everyone has to start somewhere, I had to make a deliberate choice not to reroute when someone approached me in my aisle—a choice to stay the course and at least say "Hi." Then I had to pray and persist until I began to escape my little loveless world.

To not open yourself to others is to close the door to others. This is the opposite of love. It really is true—a choice not to speak is a choice not to love. But a choice to open up is a choice to discover, and to be discovered, in ways that are more delightful every day.

I'm still learning that lesson forty years later.

DISCUSSION AND REFLECTION

1. If "to keep your heart and spirit closed does far more harm than is supposed," what do you think your next step needs to be in your top two or three most important relationships?
2. Do you find it hard to open up? Why do you think that is? What bad experiences or current fears are hindering your opening-up process?
3. Which of the suggested topics on pages 54–58 would you find the easiest to talk about? Which the hardest? Describe why you think some are harder than others.
4. Have you ever been helped when someone confronted you with their suspicions?
5. Who are the people in your life to whom you are most likely to open up? What is it about them that makes you feel comfortable doing so?

CHILL

OPEN UP

MAKE TIME

MEAN WHAT YOU SAY

UNDERSTAND WHAT YOU HEAR

NOURISH WITH GRACE

INITIATE PEACE

CELEBRATE OTHERS

ASSUME YOU ARE WRONG

THINK THE BEST

EXAMINE YOUR HEART

3

MAKE TIME

"Do two men walk together unless they have made an appointment?" (Amos 3:3 NASB)

"But exhort one another every day, as long as it is called 'today.'" (Heb. 3:13)

"And day by day, attending the temple together and breaking bread in their homes, they received their food with glad and generous hearts." (Acts 2:46)

To talk takes time, so try to plan
How much and when, as best you can.

I'm sure I wore my halibut-on-ice look the time our friends Johnny and Bonnie blamed us for the breakdown of our friendship with them. There had been months of growing distance and rising tensions between us. Little stuff—you know how it goes. Not as many invitations. Few conversations. Fewer warm hugs. Shorter answers to our questions. Less information about their lives. More distrust. Greater suspicion. Increased frustration and criticism. Deepening resentment. Even bitterness. So it continued, and thus it worsened.

Finally—and that is a key word here: *finally*—after months without meaningful conversation, we arranged to get together. We arrived at their place ready to find out why *they* had failed our friendship. But Johnny and Bonnie got to the blame game first. During our time—which is another key word: during our *time* together—they listed our offenses. Then it was our turn—only we felt more than a little sheepish, given that we had all the same gripes that they had. It would have been comical, if it weren't so painful: they had come with a long list of concerns about how we had ignored them, overlooked them, underappreciated them, mistreated them, and distanced them—and it was as if they were reading off of our script!

These things happen. As long as we humans live on this side of a perfected eternity, we will disappoint one another and then distort the facts to enable us to assign blame elsewhere, in order to stroke our own consciences and avoid our own responsibilities. Sometimes unwittingly, and sometimes with full premeditated spite, we mess up relationships and then pin the mess on somebody else.

If I were to weigh the blame objectively in our Bonnie and Johnny crisis, it would measure out pretty equally all around. The greatest offense that we all shared, though, was not what people might think. We were guilty of a mutual mismanagement of *time* long before we were guilty of a mutual misunderstanding of each other. Our relational breakdown could be traced in large measure to a failure to stay in one another's lives in meaningful and consistent ways. Trust failed because scheduling failed.

The failure to make time is a death knell to relationships. People cannot enjoy the deep and lasting love to which they've all been called—they cannot *chill* when angry, or *open up* when frustrated and hurt, or engage in any of the relationship-strengthening communication principles that follow—unless they *make time* to be with each other.

RADIO SILENCE

I recently sent off a quick note to a guy whom I've considered a friend. I had a few ideas that I thought would interest him and on which I thought he might want to weigh in. I also posed a couple of questions for him—questions that were, as it turned out, of a sensitive nature, and which got into issues of race, politics, and conservative white Christians like me. They seemed like safe thoughts and questions, given the friendship equity that I assumed we had. But I soon found out otherwise.

He replied with some direct answers to my questions, but then, to my surprise, he asked penetrating questions of his own in order to probe my intent. What bothered this brother in the Lord were what he called my seasons of "radio silence"—periods when he saw and heard neither hide nor hair from me. Absence of contact had made him feel like his concerns were not really my concerns and that I was boxing him out in favor of other priorities and people.

Long periods without conversation had stunted our relationship and generated within him suspicions of my motives. He didn't trust me as a friend, because I hadn't invested enough time and energy into him in order to earn that trust. And given that he is a black brother who has had way too many white guys come flitting into his life with all kinds of trendy racial concern, only to fly out with equal haste, he had all the more reason to doubt my authenticity.

Here's what I had to learn afresh: if this (or if any) friendship was going to become what I wanted it to become, it would need more *time*. And this time would not just happen; it would need to be *made*. We can put it like this:

> To talk takes time, so try to plan
> How much and when, as best you can.

IMAGE TO IMAGE

This need for us to schedule time with life's priority people—as God defines priority—has plenty of biblical support. First, it is expressed simply in Amos 3:3, where God asks, "Do two men walk together unless they have made an appointment?" (NASB). The obvious answer is "Of course not!" Two people cannot share a walk unless they agree on the when and the where. Hit-and-miss spontaneity in relationships can be fun, but it's highly overrated, and it usually results in spotty attention to the relationships that matter most. Every time we set a date for anything with anyone, we prove that in order for things to happen with others, we need to make time for them.

More significantly, key biblical figures spent enormous amounts of time with one another in order to develop priority relationships and disciple priority people. When Moses had conversations with God, Joshua would not leave his side (see Ex. 33:11). Elijah and Elisha were practically inseparable (see 2 Kings 2:1–2). Our Lord himself gave his disciples three solid, everyday years of his life.

Quality time with others is great, but quantity time is of first importance. The early Christians met with one another and encouraged each other *daily* (see Acts 2:46; Heb. 3:13). This significant commitment of time was the only way that the dozens of "one anothers" in Scripture—the commands to love, honor, encourage, bear with, exhort, confess sins to, pray for, teach, sing to, welcome, and greet one another—could be practiced. You cannot share life's one-another walk unless you agree on when and where to meet.

This explains why the writer of Hebrews urges us to "consider how to stir up one another to love and good works, not neglecting to meet together, as is the habit of some, but encouraging one another, and *all the more* as you see the Day drawing near" (Heb. 10:24–25). The author is saying, "Make sure to make more and more time to be together in order to do the important relational and spiritual business of New Testament church life." The life that is commanded in Hebrews 10 does not happen unless people set a time and a place and then press "Repeat."

Our heavenly Father models this best of all, as can be seen in how much time he devotes to us. His eagerness to spend time with humans, not because he needs us but because we need him, traces from Eden (see Gen. 3:8–9) into eternity—which is the ultimate and endless expression of "time." In his description of the New Jerusalem, John writes, "And I heard a loud voice from the throne saying, 'Behold, the dwelling place of God is with man. He will dwell with them, and they will be his people, and God himself will be with them as their God'" (Rev. 21:3).

The Son of God is equally committed to spending time with us. He is creating an eternal time and place so that we can be with him where he is (see John 17:24). Consider these astonishing words of Jesus: "I will come again and will take you to myself, that where I am you may be also" (John 14:3). This desire that our Savior expresses is almost too marvelous for words. He wants to be with us. So he is preparing a place where time and busyness will no longer hinder our communion with him. "No time," "Some other time," "I haven't got time," and "I wish we had more time" will not be part of the language of heaven. By his own will and for his own pleasure, Jesus will create a never-ending Today for us to enjoy together.

Such is the love of God in Christ. And such should be our love for one another—to the best of our ability in a time-bound world. Each of us needs to respect the image by *reflecting* the image. Deep communication with others is impossible without a significant godlike intentional investment of time. No God-given priority relationship in your life can survive, much less thrive, without the sharing of time. Marriage oneness. Parental love. Racial reconciliation in the church. Pastoral team unity. Sibling peace. Friendship and gospel connections with unbelievers. Be a time miser in any of these relational spheres, and the relationships won't last.

TWO SHIPS PASSING

One of the earliest opportunities I had to present this communication material was a several-year stint that I spent as a guest teacher to public high school seniors. One day, a young teacher approached me after I'd urged his students to make time for important relationships. He was concerned about his marriage, which was only a year or two old. He and his wife had quickly become the proverbial two ships passing in the night. Each of these newlyweds had leaped into full career mode, pursuing money, opportunity, and success so relentlessly that they rarely saw each other—and even more rarely spoke with each other.

I entreated him to make time with his wife to talk about how they could make more time for each other, lest they suffer the loss of their marriage. He balked a bit, clearly unsure whether either of them would be willing to sacrifice their personal goals and games. She was an ambitious career woman, and he an ambitious teacher, coach, and fitness nut. They were both committed to pursuing the inconsequential at the expense of the invaluable.

I left feeling burdened and doubtful for their future—with good reason, it turned out. When I returned to his class a year later, their marriage was over; they had divorced in less than three years. I won't pretend to know all the causes, but I do know at least one. They had failed to prioritize each other and make time for each other.

The husband-wife relationship is often at risk. Instead of investing prime energy and time in the one relationship that God intends to be the lifelong priority of those who are married, couples spend themselves on everything and everybody else. When spouses are inattentive to each other and fail to nourish their marriage, they light a fuse that will sooner or later set off an explosion.

Twenty-five months in or twenty-five years—it's only a matter of time for those who don't make enough time.

Marriage is not the only relationship that is affected by the neglect to make time, of course. All our important human connections are threatened by busyness with nonessentials, and the relationships that are closest and dearest are the most vulnerable. Usually the relationships that suffer the most are the ones that we presume on the most.

NOT UNLESS THERE'S BLOOD

In our early married life, Gayline and I saw some pastors blow up their marriages through neglect. Thankfully, I had a dad in ministry who refused to let that happen. But being a preacher's kid did give me a front-row seat to witness the time-related temptations of pastoral ministry. I remember pastors who took pride in giving in to those temptations—who wore their sacrifice of family time "for the Lord's sake" as a badge of honor. In fact, one veteran pastor counseled me early on to be so committed to pastoral ministry that my wife and kids would never know whether I'd be home for dinner or not. Horrific advice—which, thankfully, I completely ignored. Instead I decided to be home for dinner pretty much every night—unless somebody was either literally or spiritually bleeding and dying.

You may not be a pastor, but we all have pushes and pulls on our time. They may involve career advancement or soccer programs or the pressure of human need all around us. If we are not careful, people and expectations that are not God-given priorities can demand our time and drive our schedules. This means that we need to reassess our commitments periodically in order to create space and time for the people who matter most.

Gayline and I knew that if we failed to prioritize each other, we would lose each other. And when six children were added to the mix, our need for intentional time management became all the more acute. One way we made time was to lock in thirty to forty-five minutes almost every day, right after dinner cleanup. We banished the kids to the opposite end of the house to play with toys or watch a show while we sat together in quiet with our evening coffee and a bit of face-to-face time. This plan fixed relationally focused time into place for us almost every day, and it worked. That, together with blocking out longer chunks of time whenever possible, turning shopping trips into dates, getting away once in a while, and seizing every random moment we could to talk and share and love, kept us always leaning into each other.

I recommend that every couple approach their time together similarly. Craft your own plan—but make sure that you have one. And if you are not married, then consider those whose friendship is dear and whose fellowship and/or relationship is important to you, and give them the best of your time—for their good and yours.

PROXIMITY IS A PORTAL

God calls us to respect and love all those who bear his image—and that means everyone! However, this requires extra time when relationships have been strained by pride, prejudice, inequity, and injustice. We see this particularly in the area of racial reconciliation within the church. Ethnic and racial discord is no simple relational broken bone. It is a severe compound multiple fracture that cripples the human race, and it will never be healed—even in the church—unless we invest a great amount of time into reconciling and restoring. And I believe the Lord wants many more of us to do just that.

Christ came to bring us together through the blood of his cross (see Eph. 2:11–22), and he commands us to preserve this unity that he created (see Eph. 4:1–3). Yet many have observed that Sunday morning is still the most segregated time of the week in the United States, and I suspect that the same is true in any country in which color, class, and culture lines are deeply entrenched. This distance between Sunday worshipers betrays a deep underlying brokenness in the cross-cultural unity we are meant to share within the body of Christ, as well as a failure to live the gospel as Christ meant it to be lived.

Gospel-centered Christian love leaves us no valid choice but to close this distance. Justice advocate Bryan Stevenson tells us that "proximity is a portal"—a doorway leading to an opportunity. He argues that we have to bridge the gap by moving closer and making time, because closer proximity helps us to see things we've never seen before.[1] Speaker, writer, and NFL football player Benjamin Watson agrees: "Only when we share time together and *make it personal* will we lay aside the prejudice of our minds and experience the true understanding of our hearts."[2]

When we share enough time, we see things that we've never seen before. The nearer we are, the clearer we see. The more we listen, the more we learn. And the more we learn, the more we love. Intentional time—in massive amounts—is the first key step toward addressing multigenerational injustices and lifelong prejudices, no matter what part of the world we live in.

FROM MIND TO HEART

I was raised in almost all-white contexts and had very little contact with people of color, which meant that I had almost no contact with African-American believers. So when I first read extensively of the black-white divide within the church, it was abstract for me. My mind was affected, but not my heart. I learned that there was a problem, but I didn't know people who had

1. Bryan Stevenson, "Grace, Justice, and Mercy: An Evening with Bryan Stevenson and Tim Keller" (lecture, Redeemer Church, New York, NY, May 20, 2016), available online at https://www.redeemer.com/r/grace_and_race.

2. Benjamin Watson, *Under Our Skin: Getting Real about Race—and Getting Free from the Fears and Frustrations That Divide Us* (Carol Stream, IL: Tyndale Momentum, 2015), 117.

experienced that problem firsthand. And so began my commitment to pursue proximity. I asked Robert Cameron, the author of a book that had a tectonic influence on my thinking,[3] if we could be friends. Not knowing then how much courage and grace it took for him to say yes, we became friends before he passed into glory. Long conversations with Robert led to deep change in me.

That friendship led to many more—more than I can count. These have involved hundreds of hours of up-close conversation and listening—each minute of which has altered my ability to see, even when I may not agree. There is hardly a week that passes, now, when I do not read or hear comments from white folks that I know they would not make if only they would spend long hours listening to people whose life experiences have been radically different from theirs.

None of this is easy, of course. But easy has nothing to do with it. The cross on which Jesus bled out and died in order to reconcile us all to God and to one another wasn't easy. Love never is. But true understanding, peace, and reconciliation can happen no other way.[4]

WHY IS MAKING TIME SO HARD?

Whatever the relationship you are building and deepening, you will find *making time* to be very hard, even though the principle is pretty simple. In fact, it is so simple that one has to wonder why it is so hard. Two contributing factors come readily to mind.

First, the Enemy of Christ and his church has a personal interest in keeping us from making the time necessary to strengthen

3. Robert J. Cameron, *The Last Pew on the Left: America's Lost Potential* (LaFayette, LA: Prescott Press, 1995).

4. In our multicultural church, we make time for ongoing conversation by scheduling several GRACE and Race fellowships each year. For much more on this and on the need for cross-cultural proximity and time commitment, see Appendix A: GRACE and Race Fellowship.

relationships. Satan is a divider, and his demons are involved whenever disorder and selfish ambition, rather than godly wisdom and relationship, prevail (see James 3:13–18). So he will distract us from our relationship priorities with a thousand lesser pursuits. This is why, near the center of his call for us to have peace with others, James charges us to "resist the devil" (James 4:7).

Second, making time is hard work and requires deliberate and persevering effort. Ever since the fall, any effort to do anything that is worth doing has had to contend with thorns, weeds, and thistles (see Gen. 3:17–19). Nothing comes easily—and especially nothing good. Relationships require an intentional planting and watering of priority time commitments and a constant weeding of time wasters.

With that in mind, let me close this chapter with a few starter points that can help to get you on your way.

HOW TO MAKE TIME IN FIVE NOT-SO-EASY STEPS

I live my life by two good books. My Bible tells me what to do, and my old-school calendar tells me when to do it. You will need these two good books, too—or their electronic equivalents. The Bible, applied to your life through prayer and counsel, will help you to discern your priority relationships, and your calendar will help you to plan how to fit them all in.

With a calendar in hand, I encourage you to apply principle to practice, starting right now—don't stop with theory. To that end, here are five not-so-easy suggestions to get you going.

Identify your priority relationships, as God would define them. List your primary relationships and then seek to identify their order of priority, through the Word and prayer. For me, these do not include the various tasks and counseling appointments that fit into my normal pastoral Tuesday-through-Sunday hours or additional time that I need for good rest and adequate exercise. My list is as follows: Gayline, children and grandchildren, aging parents, Risen Hope co-elders and their wives, pastoral and ministry teams, small-group members, specific unbelievers I am befriending and reaching for Christ, cross-cultural friendships, men I am discipling, and a handful of personal friendships that nourish Gayline and me.

My list probably reveals how I think about priorities. I encourage you to pray (and to seek advice) to be able to find your way into your own list—perhaps using the categories of family, community, ministry, location, diversity, evangelism, and friendship.

Family	Spouse, children, grandchildren, parents, and those who have family needs of their own, such as singles, the widowed, and the fatherless.
Community	People in your church small group or in other ministry contexts whom you are called to relate to through close fellowship and care.
Ministry	Leadership and team members with whom strong relationships are important for the purpose of unity and strength.
Location	Neighbors whom you are to love—people whom God has placed next door or in the next cubicle.
Diversity	Friendships that you cultivate intentionally to diversify your circle of relationships.
Evangelism	Specific unbelievers who do not yet know Jesus and the liberty of his forgiving and transforming grace.
Friendship	People who help to balance the demands of service and ministry with the safety and security of their unconditional friendship love.

Define needs that each person has that you are responsible (or want) to provide, and then schedule time to provide each, starting with those that are most important. Define what needs your priority people may have as well as your God-given role in the meeting of those needs. Then mark your calendar with the date and time when you will do it. If you are like me, you will find it helpful to get input on this from your spouse and from wise and mature believers—especially until you are skilled in doing it yourself.

Use existing commitments and opportunities for relational multitasking. Hospitality is one great way to multitask relationally. Since you are going to eat anyway, why not make sure that the family is all together for it and that there are regular times each month when someone who's not in your family is sharing your table? Similarly, why not invite an unbelieving neighbor over to watch the game or share the BBQ? Why not turn errands into time with your children or grandchildren? It helps to figure out not only what you have to do but also whom you can do it with.

Let alternatives supplement, not substitute. Beware of letting social media replace real, person-to-person relationship. Facebook is a good supplement—especially for relationships from afar—but it is not a substitute. Texting is cool, but it's not the same as talking. Instagram can show folks a picture of your face, but your relationships will be far healthier if people see your face live, up close, and personal.[5] Video chat is a wonderful gift. How else would I be able to see my grandchildren who live hundreds of miles away? But relationships are living, breathing, organism-like experiences that draw life from actual in-person nourishment whenever possible. They cannot even survive, much less thrive, if they are screen-derived or time-deprived.

5. Tony Reinke's *12 Ways Your Phone Is Changing You* (Wheaton, IL:

Be in the moment. Making time with family doesn't always require huge commitments. Sometimes it's a simple matter of being all in, wherever we are. Being focused at dinner time around the table. Taking a fifteen-minute walk. Turning shopping into fun or a date. Pausing to look your kids in the eyes.

Of course, larger amounts of time are also needed. But the more you invest time in different types of amounts, the more you will find that two-minute moments that are attentively invested can have the relational "cash value" of a two-hour block of time.

LOST IN MY WORLD OF WORDS

When playoff time comes, I like to watch football. Having just completed another football season this weekend, I asked Gayline if she ever worried about being a football widow. She said no, but then (was it with semiserious intent?) added, "I might be more concerned about being a 'book widow.'" It's at least crossed her mind as she sees me in my chair, with my head bent toward my computer in locked concentration and my fingers racing for words, that there is relationship peril in the writing of this book. How ironic (and demonic) it would be if, while authoring a book on communication, I failed to communicate with the most wonderful person in my life.

Winston Churchill reportedly said, "Writing a book is an adventure. To begin with it is a toy, an amusement; then it becomes a mistress, and then a master and then a tyrant."[6] We all have adventures, toys, and amusements that threaten to become our mistresses, masters, and tyrants. One way to prevent them

---

Crossway, 2017) is a very helpful, balanced, and well-researched work that calls attention to the ways that technology has helped and hurt our relational lives.

6. James C. Humes, *The Wit and Wisdom of Winston Churchill: A Treasury of More Than 1000 Quotations and Anecdotes* (New York: Harper Perennial, 1995), 106.

from ever doing so is to fully devote our hearts to both making and guarding time for the ones whom we are called to love.

DISCUSSION AND REFLECTION

1. If it's true that "to talk takes time, so try to plan how much and when, as best you can," what do you need to do next?
2. Do you prefer spontaneity over planned friendship and family time? If so, describe some of the possible downsides to spontaneity.
3. Who are three significant people in your life with whom you have wanted to get together but haven't done so for a long time? How has that affected your relationships with them?
4. Create your list of priority people in your life. Check in with your spouse or a spiritually mature person to see what they think of your list.
5. Can you identify a mistress, master, or tyrant in your life—a person or hobby or job or exercise routine or project that has taken priority status away from any of your priority relationships?

CHILL

OPEN UP

MAKE TIME

MEAN WHAT YOU SAY

UNDERSTAND WHAT YOU HEAR

NOURISH WITH GRACE

INITIATE PEACE

CELEBRATE OTHERS

ASSUME YOU ARE WRONG

THINK THE BEST

EXAMINE YOUR HEART

4

MEAN WHAT YOU SAY

"Let your 'yes' be yes and your 'no' be no." (James 5:12)

"Do not lie to one another, seeing that you have put off the old self with its practices." (Col. 3:9)

"Little children, let us not love in word or talk but in deed and in truth." (1 John 3:18)

Since being heard depends on you,
Make all your words both straight and true.

Jack's Bluetooth was smoking. Flame-throwing Jill had just vented through his headset, scorching both his ear and his heart. Her final words seared his soul: *"Why don't you just bring home your paycheck and then leave?"* Jack's thoughts spun in crazy confusion; these weren't words to inspire his confidence as he prepared for the potential new client he was just minutes from seeing. But Jill could hardly be blamed for her bad timing. Jack was almost always prepping for another customer. There was hardly ever a time in between his business appointments for her to say what she wanted to say. That was the problem. He was always scoring another deal—always creating another business notch on his career belt. As a hard-driving, expensive-suit kind of guy, Jack worked long hours, and things were hopping on the career and prosperity front.

Meanwhile, Jill was home with the kids—a couple of fine and healthy little ones who gave her plenty of joy but also (as is the way with kids) tested and exhausted her limits. Jack and Jill were involved in their church when it fit their lifestyle but were not all-in when it came to faith and life in Christ. Stir in the fact that both of them were pretty loud and proud and did everything big—big style, big house, big dreams, and big fights—and the prognosis was poor by the time they arrived in my office. Their longstanding crisis wore as many layers as an Alaskan in mid-winter.

Sadly, we never got to peel off the layers, because when it seemed like Jill was telling Jack that she didn't want him to come home and stay, he didn't. They got divorced not long thereafter—a pretty clear sign that his heart never really went home again. His body may have, but he did not.

Jill's words were hot and harmful—spewed by a wife and mom who had had enough. To Jack's ears, she wanted him out; so he got out. But did she really want him out? Was she truly interested in only his money and not him? Taken at face value, her words seemed to say so.

But the truth is that she did not mean what she said. As I tried in vain to salvage their marriage, I discovered that what she had meant was not "I want you to leave" but "I want you to stay." What she meant was "Jack, you are working so much, and away from the kids and me so much, that all you really seem to be good for is a paycheck. Jack, please come home!" What she meant was "Jack, the kids and I love you and need you home with us. Won't you please put us first?"

But that is not what she said. What she said and what she meant were two different things. And while her words were by no means the sole cause of their divorce, they stoked the fire.

WHAT MEN REALLY MEAN

I have read somewhere that if a man says, "I can't find it!" what he means is "When I opened my eyes and what I was 'looking for' had not fallen magically into my outstretched arms, I had no idea what to do next!"

Earlier in our marriage, I would call out to Gayline, "Where's the ketchup?" before I even tried to find it. Never mind that she was at the other end of the house and I was in the kitchen. Without thinking about where it might be, or figuring out where it obviously was, or making the slightest effort to open the refrigerator door and look, I impulsively and ever so rudely called for help.

What did "Where's the ketchup?" really mean? It's humbling—even mortifying—to think about how clueless my conscience was when I would ask her that. Later, when the Spirit exposed my intent behind it, I saw that my real meaning was "Gayline, I would rather not exert any energy on dressing my hot dog. Will you please come and do this for me?" Even more bluntly stated, I meant this: "Gayline, I am a selfish and lazy man who, in my desire to be pampered by a doting wife, treats her with demeaning and presumptuous disrespect." That is what I really meant. I honestly wonder how she endured my selfish ways.

If you're a guy, let me just say it: it's unsettling that whenever I share this ketchup story in a mixed crowd, the men divert their eyes in uncomfortable self-awareness, while the women give me a look that says, "Preach!"

But we should know that this of course only *appears* to be a single-gender issue. If you Google "What do men/women really mean when they say the things they say?" you'll find dozens of sites devoted to funny and not-so-funny gender misspeak. We all say what we do not mean. Both genders are equally mysterious; equally silly, annoying, and sinful; equally prone to say and do the wrong things; equally guilty of saying one thing while meaning another; and, yes, equally oblivious to the damage that this inflicts. But the trouble is that when we do not say what we mean and mean what we say, a habit that may seem only silly and annoying can become toxic to a marriage, to church unity, to political discourse, to racial understanding—indeed, to any and all of our relationships.

MEAN WHAT YOU SAY

Words that are spoken without being meant are a scourge upon human relationships—a careless, sinful habit that disrespects the image of God in others, frustrates their hearts, and poisons communication. We must seek, as a matter both of law (something that God commands) and of love (something that others desire and need), for every word that we speak to be honest in every respect, accurate to our truest feelings, and as clearly expressive of what we are really thinking as possible. With much prayer and care (as well as advice), we should seek to express what we mean in the way that each moment and each relationship requires.

This is about both honesty *and* clarity. It's about meaning what we say and saying it with care and precision. Vague, cryptic, or hidden meanings are pretty much equal to lies if we have it in our power to speak what we are thinking more clearly and accurately. Integrity requires that we avoid not only false words but fuzzy ones as well, since obscure, mysterious, or backhanded words can be as damaging as any barefaced lie.

This principle is not an opportunity to justify unkindness or cruelty in the guise of telling it like it is. Other rules apply—such as our need to nourish with grace (chapter 6) and celebrate others (chapter 8). This is a call to humble integrity and clarity.

> Since being heard depends on you,
> Make all your words both straight and true.

The biblical mandate for truth-telling straight talk is clear. Using simple imperatives, such as "Do not lie to one another, seeing that you have put off the old self with its practices" (Col. 3:9) and "let your 'yes' be yes and your 'no' be no" (James 5:12), as well as solemn warnings, such as "There are . . . things that the LORD hates . . . that are an abomination to him: . . . a lying tongue . . . [and] a false witness who breathes out lies" (Prov. 6:16–17, 19), God makes his will clear. He means what he says when he tells us to mean what we say. He further commands that our talk match our walk (see 1 John 3:18), and he tells us stories about how lying and misspoken words put others at risk (see Gen. 20) and wreak havoc upon our lives (see Acts 5:1–10). We are not to vacillate between a clear yes or no, thereby obscuring our true intentions and leaving people confused and wounded (see 2 Cor. 1:17–19).

GOD SAID IT AND THAT SETTLES IT

I don't want this principle to hit you like a moralistic two-by-four. It's much richer and deeper than that. Keep in mind that the God in whose image we have all been made is wonderfully trustworthy. He can be relied on implicitly to say what he means and to mean what he says. In fact, he *cannot* lie (see Titus 1:2 NASB). With God, nothing is impossible—except sinning in general and lying in particular (see Heb. 6:17–18). This doesn't mean that we will always understand what he says, since we are only images of God—not God himself. Given our limitations, he will say and do things that are beyond our comprehension. This is inevitable, since his ways are not our ways or his thoughts our thoughts (see Isa. 55:8–9). But we can count on God to tell us whatever we need to know—straight and true, honest and clear.

A friend once owned a station wagon that sported a bumper sticker saying, "God said it. I believe it. That settles it." The sticker speaks truth, though many have suggested that it needs a slight tweak. It would be more accurate to say, "God said it. That settles it." Because it does. The fact that God said it makes it a settled reality, whether I believe it or not. God's Word doesn't need my validation in order to be true. It is true because he is true.

How much sweeter our relationship with God the Father, the Son, and the Spirit becomes the moment we understand that the Bible is his Word and that, since he cannot lie, the Bible cannot either. When we say with Jesus, "Your word is truth" (John 17:17)—and then read, hear, study, believe, love, and obey it as such—we reach a new level of intimacy and trust with our triune God. Everything that God says is true and can be trusted with implicit confidence and faith. "God is not man, that he should lie, or a son of man, that he should change his mind" (Num. 23:19). There is no need to doubt or second-guess God. God's Word is better than gold. His promises, commands, and self-revealing words and deeds are fully true and trustworthy—making the Bible the one and only book you will ever read that you never need to question or doubt. What it really says, God really means.

The same should go for us.

TWO DISCIPLINES OF THE TONGUE

Someone once asked me if it's a *sin* to be misunderstood. It's an interesting question that calls for reflection. Some misunderstandings cannot be helped. They happen because people either start with different assumptions and life experiences, or define words differently from each other, or are distracted through no fault of their own. We are limited and fallible. Little to no sin there. Yet it is a sin for us to be misunderstood *if* the misunderstanding is our fault—if we have been careless or thoughtless in how we've spoken our minds.

If we want to mean what we say and avoid the sin of being misunderstood, we need to practice two disciplines of the tongue. First, *we need to express carefully what we mean*. We shouldn't veil our thoughts with vague and mysterious words. It isn't fair to make others guess at our meaning. And whatever we do, let's not do what Jill did. Let's not say the opposite of what we mean and then hold others accountable to interpret accurately what we're trying to say.

Unless you're in a committee brainstorming meeting that welcomes smart and dumb ideas alike, make it a rule never to talk to people with unedited or ill-conceived words. Relationships in which people do that can't work. Our relationships—especially those that are in conflict or disarray—should *not* be an ill-considered, mutual free-flow of feelings, ideas, or opinions. When we *think out loud* as a way of doing marriage or racial dialogue or conflict resolution or business negotiation or parent-teen bonding, we invite misunderstanding.

Instead, we should *think in secret* and then speak out loud—and, even then, only if we can still say what we want to say after carefully checking (and, if necessary, editing) our words ahead of time. "The heart of the righteous ponders how to answer, but the mouth of the wicked pours out evil things" (Prov. 15:28). This discipline requires restraint and self-editing.

If the heart of the righteous ponders how to answer, then God wants us to be careful and intentional about every word we choose to say (or to type). An unchecked and unedited version of us will lead to misunderstanding; and, yes, it will be our fault. In such moments, it is a sin to be misunderstood.

SELF-EDITING QUESTIONS

These six questions can come in handy as we fine-tune our words:

- Are these words truthful?
- Are these words balanced (i.e., not exaggerated)?

- Are these words clarifying (i.e., not confusing)?
- Are there better words that I can use?
- How would I interpret these words if I were in the other person's shoes?
- Do my words, my tone, and my attitude all match?

The second discipline we need to practice in order to mean what we say is to *avoid words that we simply do not mean*. Too often our conversations are freighted with words that we don't mean—which we would know we don't mean if we only slowed ourselves down and assessed them. In my counseling experience, a few such words stand out as being especially common and damaging.

For instance, two words that are almost never helpful and almost always harmful are those two very words: *never* and *always*. When I hear either of these words—and I often do—I'm tempted to reference Inigo Montoya of *Princess Bride* fame and say, "I don't think that word means what you think it means." Last I checked, *never* means never—as in, not ever. And *always* means always—as in, all the time. But you would never (I mean *seldom*) know it from the way we use those terms.

A couple once came to me for counseling. In the course of conversation, the wife and I had this exchange:

> Wife: "My husband never helps me with the kids."
>
> Me: "Excuse me. I don't mean any disrespect, but I want to make sure I understand [cue chapter 5]. What do you mean by *never*? Do you mean never ever, or only once in a while, or once per month, or once per week, or not as often as you would like?"
>
> Wife: "Maybe once per day—so I guess I mean not as often as I would like."

There's a massive difference between "never" and "not as often as I would like"—a difference both in meaning and in effect. If Gayline says to me, "You never put your clothes away," instead of "I would really appreciate it if you put your clothes away more often," she has lied. The truth is that I *do* sometimes put my clothes away. Not only has she lied, she has also offended and insulted me, since I am not so big of a loser as to *never* care for her in this way.

Likewise, if an old-timer like me says that the younger generation *always* acts or thinks or speaks in a certain way, then I have not spoken the truth. If a man suggests that women never make sense, or if a woman claims that men are always jerks, such two-way stereotypes do great harm. If I categorize the actions or attitudes of ethnically diverse people in terms of what they *always* or *never* do or are like, then I have hurled both a lie and a slur. It is just this kind of stereotyped, prejudiced exaggeration that has long enflamed racial relations.

Never and *always* are the verbal equivalents of cornering a wounded animal. When they are spoken, the cornered one almost inevitably comes out snarling, clawing, and biting. Such dishonest and destructive words must be deleted from all our conflicts, or else the war of words will escalate.

Another set of words, "I'm sorry" and "That's okay," has also done untold damage. These words are misused so often and so pervasively that they have ceased to have any real meaning. Worse, they now cloak the reality of our hearts so effectively that a whole world of hurt lurks in many people, though it may not be consciously seen, felt, or faced.

Two men have a fight. They insult, demean, slander, slur, and defame each other. One curses the other out, and the other curses back with equal vim. Damage done. And there things sit for a day or week or month or year. When the feud gets too uncomfortable to bear (or, more likely, when their wives, who want to restore friendship between the couples, pester them enough), the guys have this quick exchange after church one Sunday:

Guy #1: "Hey, man—about what happened . . . yeah; I'm sorry."

Guy #2: "Hey; that's okay. We're good."

Guys #1 and 2 (muttering as they walk away): "Jerk."

Both are lying, because neither means what he is saying. The first is not really sorry—not with a godly grief that leads to repentance (see 2 Cor. 7:10). And the second is not really okay—because he remains hurt and offended by the way he was treated. Besides, as far as the apology itself, the first guy didn't even begin to offer it in a way that revealed honest contrition and confession. Their hollow exchange—which is reenacted countless times in countless relationships—is a culturally approved peace process. The problem is that it's a flat-out, two-sided lie—a truce that is built on sand.

The "I'm sorry" / "That's okay" dance step is an appealing but ineffective substitute for real confession and forgiveness—of the sort that owns sins specifically, forgives sins permanently, and restores relationships meaningfully. Biblical confession involves a grief-filled sorrow over wrongs that one has done, which leads to the specific confession of those sins along with a humble plea for forgiveness—all of which means placing oneself at the mercy of another. And biblical forgiveness is a godlike promise of pardon—a pledge that, from that moment onward, the offense that has been committed will no longer be held against the offender. It is a covenant that the relationship will now be restored to authentic love.[1]

Biblical confession and repentance mean the restoration of understanding and relationship. "I'm sorry" and "That's okay"

1. For a provocative but compelling look at the nature of true forgiveness, see Jay E. Adams, *From Forgiven to Forgiving: Learning to Forgive One Another God's Way* (Amityville, NY: Calvary Press, 1994).

mean virtually nothing at all. Even worse is that, most often, they mean the opposite of what they say. A pretend apology leads to genuine animosity. Nothing good can come when we do not mean what we say—and nothing ever will.

We could cover a much longer list of words that are commonly spoken but "not really meant"; but there's no need to dwell on the specifics. The way forward is for us to measure every word, before we say it, by the test of accuracy, clarity, and integrity. Any word that does not pass this test simply should not be spoken.

WHEN EVERYBODY'S LISTENING

Nowadays we hear and read so many ugly things (albeit things that people claim they really don't mean) that it's tempting to think that the toxicity of personal, political, racial, and gender conversations has reached unprecedented highs. But I don't think that is true. Have you ever read old political debates from previous centuries? Or have you heard that President(!) Andrew Jackson allegedly once admitted, "I have but two regrets: that I have not shot Henry Clay or hanged John C. Calhoun"? From 1830–1860 there were as many as seventy violent acts committed by members of Congress.[2] They insulted one another, maligned one another, brawled with one another, stabbed and bludgeoned one another, and even dueled to the death—all with a crazy blend of bravado and gentlemanly decorum (making sure, as the Dread Pirate Roberts would say, to "kill each other like civilized people").[3] And those times were tame compared to the

2. See Tim Murphy, "If You Think Congress Is Bad Now, You Should Hear About What Happened in 1838," *Mother Jones*, January 4, 2019, https://www.motherjones.com/politics/2019/01/congress-violence-civil-war-joanne-freeman-charles-sumner/; see also Joanne B. Freeman, *The Field of Blood: Violence in Congress and the Road to Civil War* (New York: Farrar, Straus and Giroux, 2018).

3. See "Wrestling a Giant," *The Princess Bride*, directed by Rob Reiner

ferocity that has surfaced many times throughout human history. Track the barbarity of men and women, rich and poor, masters and slaves, and you'll realize that now is not worse than ever. It has always been this bad—because we humans have always been this bad. Sad, but true.

But while the toxicity levels of our conversations may be no higher, the volume is. Evil communication wields a global megaphone these days. Social media provides us with an unprecedented ability to send our words viral with a click. It's bad enough to say things that we don't mean; it's even worse when everybody is listening in on the conversation.

It is so very easy to type out words that we would pause to soften, edit, and delete if we started to say them to someone's face. In our best, most sane moments, we really do *not* want that person dead, or believe that another person is a moron, or think that anyone actually *is* a worthless piece of garbage, or believe that someone else would do the world a favor by ending his or her life. It just makes some people feel good to say so—and to say so to as many other people as possible—all with the easy convenience of a little key labeled "Enter."

But the "Enter" door swings both ways. When it swings outward, our unfiltered words *enter* into a world of hate, thereby introducing more of what that world does not need. When the door swings back at us, the world *enters* our own poisoned relationships and conversations with a tragic excitement to *click* and *share.*

This makes the very real hatred that is in the world even worse. A lot of people *are* being honest when they post malicious and poisonous things. They mean to be mean. But such hatred is further stoked by the relentless, hateful accusations of a vicious social media world that doesn't fact- or heart-check before it goes viral. The high-voltage current of venomous lies, unfiltered

---

(1987; Beverly Hills, CA: Twentieth Century Fox Home Entertainment, 2012), DVD.

exaggerations, and not-really-true, heat-of-the-moment rants flows into electronic devices everywhere and supercharges hatred all over the planet. And the unintended consequences of these untrue and unmeant words are devastating.

I cannot help but wonder how people feel when their words end up killing someone—not just metaphorically, but literally. How does the bully feel when the suicide that he or she encouraged is discovered? How must it feel for someone who has posted viral slander that assassinates another person's character to realize that what they posted ends up being false? Or what does the wife or husband or teen feel when the private woes of their family are posted for all the world to see?

"I didn't mean it." Such are the hollow words of many a loose tongue and careless heart. "I wasn't serious." Such is the excuse copped by many a mocking and cruel bully. "I was only joking." Such is the empty defense of the unthinking mind, the unfeeling heart, the unedited tongue, and the unchecked post.

> Like a madman who throws firebrands, arrows, and death
> is the man who deceives his neighbor
> and says, "I am only joking!" (Prov. 26:18–19)

"That's not what I meant." Such is the too-late tagline that is attached to the thoughtless and untrue words that we humans speak. Though we were made to reflect the life-affirming image of the one who is the Father of clarity and truth, we all too often mirror the murderous intent of the father of distortion and lies (see John 8:44).

Serious stuff. And it's all so very sad. May it be that, in the name of the Jesus whom we profess to love, we will be done with it all. And may we all, with loving and careful hearts, make sure to mean what we say—and then keep it to the ones who need to know. And if we have sinned, may we confess it to God and to others, with the assurance of his forgiveness and in the hope of theirs.

YES AND AMEN

More than once in this chapter, two paths have converged, and I want to make sure that you've noticed.

Path one: God means what he says and keeps all his promises. "For all the promises of God find their Yes in [Christ]. That is why it is through him that we utter our Amen to God for his glory" (2 Cor. 1:20). His promises are Yes in Christ. No *ifs* or *maybes.* He has given his word, and he means it. If we are in Christ by faith (meaning that he is our Redeemer, Mediator, and Righteousness before God) then all God's promises are for us; and they are sure and certain—allowing us to utter a loud and happy "Amen!"

Path two: one of the promises that God will most certainly keep is his promise to forgive.

> If we confess our sins, he is faithful and just to forgive us our sins and to cleanse us from all unrighteousness. . . .
>
> My little children, I am writing these things to you so that you may not sin. But if anyone does sin, we have an advocate with the Father, Jesus Christ the righteous. He is the propitiation[4] for our sins. (1 John 1:9; 2:1–2)

As we explore God's communication commands in the following chapters, let me echo Robert Murray McCheyne's oft-quoted words: "For every one look at yourself, take ten looks at Christ."[5] This counsel is wise. Be sure that for every hour in which you reflect on your broken promises and failed words, you take ten hours to bask in the promises that your Father has made to you—he who covenants to love us all forever and to remember our sins no more (see Heb. 10:15–17). Let these sure and certain

4. The atoning sacrifice that takes away God's wrath.

5. Andrew Bonar, *Memoir and Remains of the Rev. Robert Murray McCheyne* (repr., Carlisle, PA: Banner of Truth, 1966), 293.

promises both assure your heart before God and also inspire you to reflect his faithful, promise-keeping, and truth-telling grace to others.

DISCUSSION AND REFLECTION

1. If "Being heard depends on you, [so] make all your words both straight and true" is sound counsel, then what can you do to get started?
2. Are you a think-before-you-speak person or a speak-and-then-think person? How would your family and friends answer that question about you?
3. Describe your last instance of the "apology" and "forgiveness" process with someone. Did it measure up to the process of confession and forgiveness that this chapter described? If so, how? If not, how not?
4. What are better words to use than *never* and *always*?
5. Share your thoughts about the author's concern regarding the social media megaphone. Do you agree with that concern?

CHILL

OPEN UP

MAKE TIME

MEAN WHAT YOU SAY

UNDERSTAND WHAT YOU HEAR

NOURISH WITH GRACE

INITIATE PEACE

CELEBRATE OTHERS

ASSUME YOU ARE WRONG

THINK THE BEST

EXAMINE YOUR HEART

5

UNDERSTAND WHAT YOU HEAR

"A fool takes no pleasure in understanding, but only in expressing his opinion." (Prov. 18:2)

"If one gives an answer before he hears, it is his folly and shame." (Prov. 18:13)

To listen, cover mouth with hand
And bend your ear to understand.

I was a few months into pastoral work when Ted, a man in our church, retired from forty years of working for our very small town. I wanted to make sure that our little congregation of twenty (yes, that was about the size of it) honored him in his moment. So we planned a party. Cake. Commendations. A nice gift. All in all, it seemed like we did things up quite nicely for him. Surely he had to be pleased, and I assumed that everyone else was too—until I overheard one woman in our congregation saying to another, "They should have done more for him."

This was not the note of affirmation I was looking for. That she would judge my actions this way seemed both unreasonable and unjust. Low-grade bitterness began gnawing at my heart. While no one except the most perceptive observers would have known it, I constructed a wall of ridiculous self-pity between this critic and me.

The wall remained in place for many weeks until I overheard her again. She was still worked up over the same issue, but I heard something new this time around: "The *town* should have done more for him." One word made all the difference. She was miffed that our *town*, Ted's forty-year employer, had done so little for his retirement. My self-pity traced to an absurdly adolescent misinterpretation. She hadn't faulted me at all. My misunderstanding of her intent was due to a complete lack of effort on my part *to* understand. I had nearly destroyed a relationship by assuming that my interpretation was correct, by presuming that I had heard rightly, by failing to understand accurately what someone had said.

BACK TO JACK AND JILL

Think back to Jack and Jill, from the previous chapter. Their marriage ended, in part, due to words that Jill had not meant. She shared real blame for their divorce because she hadn't meant what she'd said. But blame must be assigned to both sides, here. Pin some on Jack too. In addition to his career idolatry, which wreaked family havoc, his failed commitment to understanding factored in, as well. What he thought Jill had meant by her words was not what she had actually meant. And while she bore responsibility for words that were carelessly chosen, he bore responsibility for words that were carelessly heard. He shared blame for not probing to discover what Jill did, in fact, mean by her words.

Laboring to understand is the way of humility and love.

> A fool takes no pleasure in understanding,
>   but only in expressing his opinion.

If one gives an answer before he hears,
it is his folly and shame.
. . . .
An intelligent heart acquires knowledge,
and the ear of the wise seeks knowledge. (Prov. 18:2, 13, 15)

It is prejudice, it is arrogance, it is folly when we draw conclusions and express opinions before we fully understand.

> To listen, cover mouth with hand
> And bend your ear to understand.

RESPECT RIGHT UP TO HERE

Andrew and I sipped our coffees one Tuesday morning. We opened our time on a casual note. As we chatted, I listened carefully, asked questions, probed for understanding, and showed real interest. Ninety minutes flew by as I asked him about his life, his journeys, his family, his faith (which was different from mine), his challenges, and his hardships. Though we disagreed on various points, he was fascinating and exuded dignity. We chatted it up some more, peeled back a few more layers, shared a few laughs, touched on a few issues, wrestled with a couple of mysteries, and even addressed some sin concerns.

When I encouraged, he smiled. When I understood his point, he was grateful. When I empathized, he was appreciative. When I asked his opinion, he gave it. When I offered him mine, he received it. When I commended how well he knew his faith, he lit up. When I disagreed, he respected my perspective. When I gave him some advice (since he had asked for it), he gave me his attention. When I offered to meet him again, he promised that it would happen. In fact, tomorrow we're going to a ball game together.

Andrew and I have lived in two different worlds while occupying the same one. As a recent immigrant from sub-Saharan

Africa, he has often felt the pain of being misunderstood and prejudged. That he is a black African and I am a white American means that he and I experience life differently in this country. Because his melanin levels are higher than mine, his advantages are lower. Although his life experiences are broader than mine, his opportunities are narrower. Though he has more courage than I, he has received less honor. And even though his yearning to be treated with dignity is equal to mine, his experience of receiving such treatment no doubt lags far behind mine. Two different worlds within the same world.

But Andrew and I are both made in the image of God—which means that he deserves my respectful, attentive, and understanding care. As I applied this truth consciously to our conversation, he opened up, and within minutes our two different worlds were aligning more closely. *Friendship happened because understanding happened. Understanding happened because respect happened.*

Andrew's closing words are what I will long remember. Emotion filled his voice as he verbalized his thoughts: "Tim, where I come from, we know when we are respected." And then, paralleling his hand to the floor and raising it slowly from his heart to his eyes, he added, "And when we are, we feel it from here right up to here." No more words were spoken. None were needed. What he was feeling at eye level was obvious. And it was mutual. Immortals had just met over coffee.

Respecting the image means that we cannot presume to understand, or rush to judge, or choose to stereotype anyone who is made in that image. Superficial hearing and prejudicial assumptions profane the dignity—the profound sanctity—of human life. If we prejudge or dismiss lightly the words of another, we commit relational violence against someone who bears vestiges of the Holy. Revering God means that we must strive to understand those who bear his image.

Sometimes I am so oblivious that I forget to clean my glasses. There have been times when Gayline has come from across the room to clean them for me. She can see from ten feet away what I don't even notice, even though my glasses are resting on my nose. Without her cleaning and clarifying work, I would keep seeing through smears and smudges—all the while thinking that I was seeing clearly.

This happens all too often in our relationships; we think we see, we think we've heard, we think we understand, we think we get it, we think we know. But we don't. Our glasses are smudged, and we don't even realize it. As someone has said, "I know that you believe you understand what you think I said, but I'm not sure you realize that what you heard is not what I meant."

HUMAN COMPLEXITY

Our difficulty with understanding one another is complicated by the fact that we're champs and chumps at the same time. Look at what the apostle Paul has to say in Romans:

> For when Gentiles, who do not have the law, by nature do what the law requires, they are a law to themselves, even though they do not have the law. They show that the work of the law is written on their hearts, while their conscience also bears witness, and their conflicting thoughts accuse or even excuse them. (Rom. 2:14–15)

> I have the desire to do what is right, but not the ability to carry it out. For I do not do the good I want, but the evil I do not want is what I keep on doing. . . .
>
> So I find it to be a law that when I want to do right, evil lies close at hand. (Rom. 7:18–19, 21)

Theologians differ on whether Romans 7 is describing believers or unbelievers. Some argue that Paul must be speaking as a believer, because in verse 18 he says that he has "the desire to do what is right." This, they argue, can't possibly describe spiritually dead unbelievers, since they have no real desire to do good. But others say that he must be describing his former life as an *un*believer, because in verse 14 of that chapter he says that he is "of the flesh, sold under sin." And this, they reason, can't possibly describe regenerated believers, in whom is the new life of the Spirit.

I propose that these phrases may describe both believers *and* unbelievers. Because the image is in everyone, everyone who has ever walked the planet has known right from wrong and had some desire to do the right and not do the wrong—but has then (except for Jesus) done the wrong anyway. You don't have to be born again in order to have a sense of right and wrong and to feel a pang of guilt when you get it wrong. This is why those who are not believers have what Paul calls "conflicting thoughts" (Rom. 2:15). Sometimes the unregenerate feel good about themselves; sometimes they do not. Sometimes they say things like "I hate myself when I treat people that way" or "That's a part of me that I wish wasn't there." And sometimes they feel satisfaction because they make a good choice.

Believers have a similar, but even greater, sense of right and wrong that makes them feel the conflict between the new them and the old them even more intensely. Elsewhere, Paul writes, "The desires of the flesh[1] are against the Spirit, and the desires of the Spirit are against the flesh, for these are opposed to each other, to keep you from doing the things you want to do" (Gal. 5:17). Paul isn't saying that we have two natures—like Jesus, who has a divine *and* a human nature. But he is saying that when it comes to being human, things are complicated.

Even if you disagree with my understanding of Romans 7, perhaps you can agree with my assessment of human experience. We simultaneously have a desire for good *and* a propensity for

1. Which include sins in the area of communication, such as enmity, strife, fits of anger, dissensions, and divisions (see Gal. 5:20).

evil. We say things that we mean on one level, while also not meaning them on another, at the same time. We speak hatefully to people we actually love. We belittle people whom we deeply revere. Sometimes our hearts want to be cruel *and* kind simultaneously, and in any given moment we can let the cruel win out. Naturally, this leaves others confounded and confused and makes the task of understanding what we hear all the more challenging.

A GOD WHO GETS US

None of this confounds God, however. Our Father above understands us, even when our words scream pain and confusion. We see this in the Psalms, which are honest cries from hurting saints—ancient hymns and prayers that are raw with reality. The Psalms hold a prominent place in Scripture, even though (or is it *because*?) they are filled with sometimes shockingly fearful, hurt, confused, angry, depressed, and even unbelieving cries from godly people in an ungodly world. Even though the ancient songwriters seem sometimes to question and second-guess God, God seldom rebukes them. Clearly, God understands something that is not easily discerned (at least by us)—the true *meaning* of their cries. He hears the heart of what the psalmists are saying through the noise of their grieving and wailing words. He understands what he hears.

This reminds me of how God distinguished between Zechariah's and Mary's responses to their respective angelic announcements. Each of them received word of a miraculous birth. Neither birth was possible by any natural means, making Zechariah and Mary's responses perfectly understandable. Zechariah asked, "How shall I know this? For I am an old man, and my wife is advanced in years" (Luke 1:18). Meanwhile, Mary responded, "How will this be, since I am a virgin?" (Luke 1:34).

Their words seem very similar. But Zechariah is disciplined by God for his doubt (see v. 20), while Mary receives no rebuke at all. If anything, she gets an angelic hug of reassurance (see vv. 35–37). What is the difference? It is one that a discerning ear, or an all-seeing eye, can detect—and God's did.

Even though Zechariah had heard an angel from God, he still wondered how he could know that the miracle would happen. There was a doubt in his mind. In contrast, Mary had no doubt—she knew that the miracle would happen and wondered only *how*. Zechariah questioned God's Word and ability; Mary questioned God's logistics. Zechariah questioned *whether* it would happen; Mary wondered *how* it would happen. Zechariah doubted and disbelieved. Mary wanted more information. And God, who can always tell, understood the difference. How humbled (and glad) we should be by the realization that God understands us! He gets us. Accurately. Fully. Sympathetically. Profoundly.

THE HUMBLE, HARD WORK OF GODLIKE HEARING

Godly communication and listening should aim for understanding—at least to the degree that fallible humans with partial knowledge can achieve it. In chapter 1, verses 16–25 of his letter, James teaches us how to hear the "word of truth" (v. 18). He wants us to rightly "receive . . . the implanted word" (v. 21) and to make sure that we *do* God's Word once we have heard it (see v. 22). In other words, there is a right way to hear preaching and teaching: "Know this, my beloved brothers: let every person be quick to hear, slow to speak, slow to anger" (James 1:19).

This can also apply to how we hear one another. He is describing a hearing that brings understanding. It is a hearing that restrains reactions and receives what people say with careful attention to what they mean.

God knows with perfect intuition. We, however, can know only through imperfect investigation—and this requires tireless and selfless effort. Dr. Martin Luther King Jr. said, "Human progress never rolls in on wheels of inevitability. It comes through the tireless efforts and the persistent work of dedicated individuals."[2] And what he said about racial healing goes for all relational healing. Understanding never "rolls in on wheels of inevitability." It is carried in and forward on the tireless shoulders of human beings—especially humans in whom genuine faith and the love of Christ abound. Understanding takes effort, patience, endurance, and a refusal to quit—whether it happens in the boardroom, bedroom, courtroom, playroom, chatroom, or newsroom. We do not come to understand our spouse or child or fellow pastor or church member or hyphenated neighbor or political opponent by hearing and defining their words with Merriam-Webster in hand. It's harder than that. We have to hear *them*.

In the rules for a debate in ancient Greece, before a person could answer his opponent's opinion, he had to repeat it in his own words—in a way that his opponent would approve. Only then could he respond. It's interesting that, even in a culture that had little to no knowledge of Christ, people would give each other such respect. Theologians call this "common grace"—a moral awareness that all people share. In this case, the ancient Greeks had an awareness of their need to respect one another's meaning. Such careful listening in order to understand will happen only if we share that same respect. And we who know the love of Christ should share and show it more than anyone else does.

LOWERING THE BUCKET

This is hard. Listening in order to gain understanding involves not only careful attention to words, tone, emotion, and body language but also follow-up that aims for clarification. "The purpose in a man's heart is like deep water, but a man of understanding

2. Martin Luther King Jr., "Remaining Awake through a Great Revolution" (commencement address, Oberlin College, Oberlin, Ohio, June 14, 1965).

will draw it out" (Prov. 20:5). People are deep wells—they have thoughts and opinions that are stored far below the surface. Sadly, these depths will remain hidden to most—unplumbed except by the few wise and discerning people who know how to draw them out. We have to be wise in order to gain understanding. With honest and humble effort we must draw out of people's hearts what they are really thinking and saying.

To that end, wise and clarifying questions will certainly be needed. What does a parent mean when he says to his teen, "You never" or "You always"? What does the wife mean when she says that her husband is so "frustrating"? What does the husband mean when he says that his wife is "cold"? What does the single person mean by the words "I feel so alone, even in a crowd"? What does the wife mean when she says that she doesn't "feel safe" around her husband? What do people mean when they say that they feel "unappreciated"?

What do different church members mean when they use the terms *white privilege* or *racist* or *disadvantaged*? What do theologians mean when they argue for or against "social justice"? Are the different people who use this term even talking about the same thing? Do I understand what they mean before I critique them?

Police shootings of black Americans have exposed that Americans have very divergent perspectives on crime and law enforcement. Opinions are loud and strong, as is clear in the urban suburb in which I live. Residents here post lots of front-yard signage. Some yards proclaim, "Black lives matter," while others say, "We support the police." In virtually everyone's minds, these two signs signal disagreement. But do they? What do people mean when they say things like this? I need to ask before I draw conclusions. If I assume that everyone who says "Black lives matter" is against the police or for a radical left agenda, I'd be wrong. If I assume that everyone who posts a "We support the police" sign doesn't care about black lives and thinks that police can do no wrong, I would again be mistaken.

If I presume to know, I will fail to understand. And if I want to know for sure, I am going to have to *ask*—person-to-person and face-to-face. The truth is that many who say "Black lives matter" respect the police highly and embrace conservative morals. And many who say "We support the police" care deeply about black lives. But you would never know this by watching TV or reading Facebook. I happen to know it because I've talked with and asked many dozens of real people who have told me so.

CLARIFYING QUESTIONS

- What did/do you mean when you said . . . ?
- I'm not sure I understood what you meant by that word. Could you explain it, please?
- How does the concern that you just expressed make you feel?
- I think I'm hearing you say this: . . . Am I right? Is that how you would say it?
- Can I try to put what you've said into my own words?
- Do you feel like there is anything you're saying that I am not yet hearing?
- Can you give me specific examples of what you are perceiving or thinking so I can be sure to understand?

CLEANING OUR GLASSES

Such a commitment to understand others is very hard in any relationship. Gender to gender. Parent to child. Old to young. Rich to poor. Highly educated to undereducated. Artsy to nerdy. Jock to klutz. Married to unmarried. Add in all the in-between and back-and-forth combinations of the above, and you sense the challenge. Factor in profound ethnic differences and cultural preferences, and the challenge often feels too daunting even to try.

These challenges can lead to partiality and prejudice, which are like greasy fingerprints on our glasses. They distort how we see people, leading us to prefer our kind—whoever they may be. But to think that any "type" is preferable to or better than or higher than or superior to any other is to run directly counter to the heart of God, who is not partial to any (see Acts 10:28, 34–35; James 2:9). Such partiality must die. It is a sinful equivalent of having badly smudged glasses—and then refusing to wipe them clean. When we look at others with our glasses smudged with bias and prejudice, we see them as less than they are—less human, less beautiful, less valuable, less worthy of our time and attention. And as a result, we do not respect them—nor will we ever understand them.

Our church holds periodic Grace and Race Fellowships as a collective effort to clean our glasses. We believe that we cannot make peace with those whom we do not understand. So these gatherings open the door for conversations that help us to see and empathize with the very real angst, fear, anger, and pain of others. I won't lie to you—these conversations are incredibly hard, and we all wish that they were no longer needed. It's no fun processing raw fears and tears—especially without the full closure of agreement and healing.[3] But, as Pastor Bryan Loritts tells us, our ability to "continue down the path of transformation, openness, and compassion" depends on our "commitment to immerse [ourselves] in the narratives of others, of people who [are] different from [us]."[4] In all our relationships, we have to realize that while God doesn't expect us all to agree, he does expect

3. See Appendix A for further information about our Risen Hope Church GRACE and Race Fellowship and for a sampling of ways in which people within our congregation have come to a new understanding of one another.

4. Bryan Loritts, *Right Color, Wrong Culture: The Type of Leader Every Organization Needs to Become Multiethnic* (Chicago: Moody Publishers, 2014), 195.

us all to understand. We have to immerse ourselves in other people's lives.

GOLDEN-RULE LISTENING

Who is it in your life whom you just don't get? Golden-Rule love makes every effort to listen and learn—since that is exactly what we want others to do for us (see Matt. 7:12). We should not assume anything in any conversation that we ever have with anyone. Nor should we trust our first impressions or interpretations or opinions or impulses to give advice. Jackie Hill Perry has it right when she says, "Being impressed with your own advice will most likely make you a terrible listener. You'll only listen up until the point that you have a great idea. Then you'll interrupt. I mean interject; so that you can share your idol. I mean your wisdom."[5]

By asking good questions before giving quick answers, we can seek understanding. May this be our implied, if not stated, commitment in all our relationships: "I am going to listen to you right now better than you have ever been listened to in your whole life. I am going to make you feel like you're the most understood person in the world. . . . I am going to [commit] 100 percent of my attention and all the love of which I am capable, strictly and solely to focus on understanding you now."[6]

Then, with our assumptions silenced, our phones turned off, our TVs darkened, our books closed, our advice restrained, and the floor relinquished, let us look into each other's eyes and—for as long as it takes us to understand—give one another our undivided attention and hearts.

5. Jackie Hill Perry (@JackieHillPerry), Twitter, May 29, 2019, 1:46 p.m., https://twitter.com/jackiehillperry/status/1133837064972189697?lang=en.

6. William M. Fletcher, *The Second Greatest Commandment: A Call to a Personal and Corporate Life of Caring* (Colorado Springs: NavPress, 1983), 88.

DISCUSSION AND REFLECTION

1. "To listen, cover mouth with hand and bend your ear to understand." Why do we find this so hard to do?
2. Is there a specific type of relationship in which understanding someone else seems hard to you (for example, old to young, rich to poor, educated to less educated, male to female, or black to white)? Why do you think it feels that way?
3. Have you ever been surprised by the raw emotion and desperate cries of the Psalms and wondered why God seems to receive these things without rebuke? What do you think this says about God?
4. What are some things you do not understand about your spouse or your pastor or your neighbor who is different from you? Are you willing to seek understanding with this person?
5. Do the clarifying questions that are provided in this chapter for drawing out understanding seem like they will be helpful? Who is one person you can try them out on this week?

CHILL

OPEN UP

MAKE TIME

MEAN WHAT YOU SAY

UNDERSTAND WHAT YOU HEAR

NOURISH WITH GRACE

INITIATE PEACE

CELEBRATE OTHERS

ASSUME YOU ARE WRONG

THINK THE BEST

EXAMINE YOUR HEART

6

NOURISH WITH GRACE

"Let no corrupting talk come out of your mouths, but only such as is good for building up, as fits the occasion, that it may give grace to those who hear." (Eph. 4:29)

"The lips of the righteous feed many." (Prov. 10:21)

"The Lord bless you and keep you." (Num. 6:24)

The gladness of relationships
Is nourished by your grace-filled lips.

I have always liked building things. It's a pleasure that I probably inherited from my dad, who, in addition to being a missionary and pastor for over fifty years, was a lifelong builder. And so, several years ago, my youngest son and I decided to build a shed, even though we didn't have any money to spend on it. As a world-class scrounger, I began to trash-pick all the materials for our shed. It took about a year for me to salvage everything that we needed for a ten-by-ten structure that was envisioned to stand some twelve or so feet at its peak. Two-by-fours, plywood, windows, shelving, siding, roof shingles, and other people's scraps and castoffs all became my supply trove. All that I actually bought were nails.

When you don't have much clue what you're doing, you need all the nails you can get.

I didn't have a real blueprint. Equipped with only a rough picture in my head, some memories of how my dad used to fit things together, a few primitive tools, and all those nails, my son and I got to it. A few weeks later, he and I pounded in the last of the nails and stood back to look at what we had made. It wasn't pretty, but it was strong. Actually, the outside didn't look half bad. The inside, however, didn't look even close to half good. Still, the job was done, the fun was had, and the shed stood strong—though I preferred that no one but immediate family ever get a good look at it.

Gayline had other ideas. She was strangely proud of her hubby and son's work and was all too happy to show it off. Imagine my dismay on the day when, through my workshop window, I saw Gayline leading Ed out to take a look at the Shorey shed. Ed was a master craftsman who wielded wood and tools like an absolutely brilliant artist. There was literally no one on earth who I wanted to see that shed *less* than Ed. But there was my dear wife leading him out to show off my work. The long, plaintive "Noooooooooo!" from my woodshop was too far off for her to hear.

I watched as Ed stood and looked, opened the shed door, stepped in, paused, looked some more, and then slowly walked back to the house. I was so mortified that I didn't even show my face. Gayline told me later that when he stood in the shed, he spoke but one word: "Interesting." That was it. *Interesting*. My only consolation is that he didn't recommend a dozer.

To my credit, my shed proved to be both interesting *and* strong. Not long after, when Hurricane Sandy blew through our New Jersey town and took down ten mighty oaks all around that shed—including one that landed against it—the shed stood firm. Built to last—even if not built for looks.

BUILDING UP WITH NOURISHING WORDS

It is good to build relationships that are interesting, too. The right kind of *interesting* is a delight. But it is also good for us to build relationships that edify and nourish so that others may become strong and beautiful through them.

So far we've been discussing basic communication logistics more than we have content. No positive communication can happen unless we make the commitment to chill, open up, make time, mean what we say, and understand what we hear. But what exactly should we *say* once these logistics are worked out? Words matter. They are essential tools and materials with which we construct the life we live together with others. That being the case, if we want our relationships to be beautiful, living, interpersonal creations that reflect the spiritual and relational craftsmanship of God, we need to choose our words well.

Life in community—in the home, the church, and the world—requires people who bear the image to be edified, or, to change metaphors, to be built up and nourished. We need words that strengthen and nourish—words that feed the soul with truth and beautify other people with grace. The Lord tells us to "encourage one another and build one another up" (1 Thess. 5:11) and to "let [our] speech always be gracious, seasoned with salt" (Col. 4:6). His Word tells us that "the lips of the righteous feed many" (Prov. 10:21) and that "gracious words are like a honeycomb, sweetness to the soul and health to the body" (Prov. 16:24).

In a classic text that ought to inform the content of our communication, Paul says, "Let no corrupting talk come out of your mouths, but only such as is good for building up, as fits the occasion, that it may give grace to those who hear" (Eph. 4:29). This is an absolutely categorical command that comes with no exceptions—and it has both a negative and a positive side.

First, "let *no* corrupting talk come out of your mouths." Paul means what he says. No means no. We are not to let any corrupting talk happen. And if you're thinking that Paul is forbidding dirty jokes and bathroom humor per se, you are missing his main point. Dirty jokes and bathroom humor are inappropriate and would be included in what Paul forbids, as is clear later on in Ephesians 5:4. But they are not his main focus here. In fact, the translation of this term as "corrupting" is a little misleading.

Here Paul uses a word that is used elsewhere for fish that have no nourishment or cash value—*worthless* fish that are fit only to be thrown back into the water. The Holy Spirit is telling us to remove all worthless, good-for-nothing talk from our conversations. We are to avoid any talk that has no edifying or nourishing value. If our words are not replenishing and edifying—or "true, kind, and necessary," as my old Sunday school teachers used to put it—they must not be spoken.

Then Paul flips to the positive side and commands the things that we *are* to say: "only such as is good for building up, as fits the occasion, that it may give grace to those who hear." Notice the filter through which we should pour our words in order to strain out unhelpful matter before we speak.

THE GRACE FILTER

- Will my words build up?
- Do they fit the occasion?
- Are they useful?
- Are they well-timed and appropriately suited to a present need?
- Are they crafted to give grace right now, right here, to the person right in front of me?

Quite the opposite of being corrupt and worthless, our words are to nourish, heal, and feed—to bring strength and blessing to those who hear.

> The gladness of relationships
> Is nourished by your grace-filled lips.

THE NOURISHING WORDS OF GOD

We respect the image in others by imitating the Speaking One in whose image we ourselves are made. There is no better way to speak with nourishing grace than to mirror the One whose words strengthen the heart, infusing health and well-being into weary and worn-out souls. Countless believers have found God's written Word to be a daily source of replenishing help and renewing strength. Since it is living, active, and abiding (see Heb. 4:12; 1 Peter 1:23), God's Word gives life to all who hear or read it in faith (see James 1:18, 21; 1 Peter 1:23; 2:2–3). It fortifies the soul.

The psalmists love to extol the replenishing value of God's Word and words. Psalm 19 includes one such celebration.

> The law of the Lord is perfect,
> reviving the soul;
> the testimony of the Lord is sure,
> making wise the simple;
> the precepts of the Lord are right,
> rejoicing the heart;
> the commandment of the Lord is pure,
> enlightening the eyes. (vv. 7–8)

God's words are perfect, sure, right, and pure; and, as such, they revive, make wise, rejoice, and enlighten.

These descriptions of how God communicates with us suggest

some helpful questions we can use to assess our words before we go on to communicate with others. Call it the *Psalm 19 Test.*

Are My Words . . .	**Will My Words . . .**
Perfect—are they complete, mature, and well-considered?	*Revive*—will they restore life, hope, and strength?
Sure—are they verified, proven, true, and faithful to the unfailing Word of God?	*Make Wise*—will they give discernment, insight, and skill in the area of applying God's Word?
Right—are they straight and upright, and do they conform to what is right and just?	*Give Joy*—will they fill hearts with God's soul-satisfying goodness?
Pure—are they untainted by sinful content or my own agenda?	*Enlighten*—will they shine light into lives that are darkened by sorrow and sin?

It goes without saying that no one but God can say everything perfectly, but that does not mean that we can speak carelessly and with untested words. If the words I want to say fail the assessment above, which is meant to ensure that they edify and nourish, then I am better off not speaking or posting or texting or messaging them.

Of course, it would be simplistic to suggest that there are no other questions for us to ask about the things we plan to say. For example, we may have to ask, "What words are *needed,* even if they are not wanted?" Edifying words do not always have to be easy to hear. Paul, Jesus, and nearly every prophet in history have spoken corrective and even rebuking words—sometimes naming names as they've done so. But we should test words like this by examining our goal behind saying them. Are we saying what we are saying in order to edify and nourish? Are we motivated by love? There are times when words that revive, make wise, and enlighten may hurt—at least in the moment. But if wounding words need to be spoken, let's make sure that they are the wounds *of a friend* (see Prov. 27:6).

And let's make sure that our words are spoken with our specific audience in mind. What we say nourishes only if it is catered to the diet of the person to whom we are speaking. Check for allergies first. Weak people are allergic to stern words. Soft words do not nourish willfully sinful people. Discouraged and grieving people will not be fortified by rebukes and stiff-upper-lip admonitions. More than once Paul urges us to employ different types of words and methods, depending on the one(s) to whom we are talking. In 1 Thessalonians 5:14, he says, "We urge you, brothers, admonish the idle, encourage the fainthearted, help the weak, be patient with them all." Some need admonishment, some need encouragement, some need help, some need comfort—and all need patience.

In 1 Timothy 5:1–2, Paul says,

> Do not rebuke an older man but encourage him as you would a father, younger men as brothers, older women as mothers, younger women as sisters, in all purity.

Some need son-to-father reverence, some need child-to-mother respect, some need brother-to-brother directness, some need brother-to-sister (or sister-to-brother) purity. *None* need impatience or attacks or judgmental self-righteousness. Our goal must be the same in every case: to nourish with our words—though the menu of words that we provide will depend on the needs of the person in that moment. "To make an apt[1] answer is a joy to a man, and a word in season, how good it is!" (Prov. 15:23).

1. That is, appropriate for the time, place, and person—well-suited for the moment.

Our words need to be an extension of a whole lifestyle that is committed to blessing others. Years ago, Christian radio speaker Robert A. Cook would close out his five-minute morning devotional with the same words every day: "Walk with the King today, and be a blessing." I heard that when I was twenty, and I remember it forty years later. It remains a simple, beautiful, and doable ambition for every day of our lives. Being a blessing in this way starts with words. It is a worthy goal for us to converse with people in such a way that they walk away from us feeling more grace than they had when they met us.

SEIZING OUR SNEEZING

I grew up in a time when a lot of Christians refused to say "God bless you" when others sneezed. Their refusal had to do with the supposed origins of this old custom. No one knows for sure why people started responding to sneezes with a quick prayer of blessing. The story I grew up with (which was the reason that we didn't say "God bless you") is that back in the day, superstitious folks thought that sneezing forced evil spirits out of the body, which prompted well-wishers to pray a quick blessing over the sneezer as a spiritual shield to block the demon from returning.[2] Lest they take part in such superstition, a lot of Christians chose to ignore sneezes rather than to bless them.

Nowadays, no one that I know superstitiously connects sneezing to a self-induced exorcism, which means that there's no good reason not to answer a sneeze with a blessing (not that there ever was). And the fact is that there is always good reason

2. Another theory is that ancients feared that a sneeze could accidentally eject the soul from the body—an unfortunate occurrence that would be worthy of a blessing, to be sure. Others suggest that the "God bless you" ritual started during one of the plagues, when sneezing was a symptom of having the plague and the means by which it spread to others. Every sneeze hinted at serious illness, which inspired folks to pray a blessing over the sneezer.

to nourish others with a blessing. So if it reminds me to pray that others be blessed, I should feel free to thank God for sneezes and then to seize each sneeze for this good and kind purpose.

The point is that blessings are good. They are words that nourish—and isn't that what our tongues are meant to do? In James 3:10, James commands us to bless rather than curse one another. The word that James uses for "blessing" is *eulogia*. It's made up of two smaller words: *eu*, which means "good" or "well," and *logia*, which means "word." It's the word from which we get *eulogy*—a speech or expression of good thoughts and words about others, usually when they have died. James's point is that we should be expressing good thoughts and wishing good things for others while they are still alive.

MAY THE LORD BE WITH YOU

We can blend the blessings that we speak to others with benedictions, as well, to create a fragrant expression of biblical faith and relationship. A benediction is a prayer—often at the beginning or end of a gathering or a letter—that seeks the good of another. The word, as we saw with *eulogia*, is a compound word that is composed of two smaller words: *bene*, which means "well," "well-being," or "good," and *diction*, which means "say" or "word."

If you have never admired the beauty of benedictions before, let me include several biblical benedictions here. I think you will sense their aroma of nourishing beauty and grace. As you read them, consider the strengthening value that they could have in your relationships.

> May the Lord give strength to his people! May the Lord bless his people with peace! (Ps. 29:11)

> May God be gracious to us and bless us and make his face to shine upon us. (Ps. 67:1)

May the God of endurance and encouragement grant you to live in such harmony with one another, in accord with Christ Jesus, that together you may with one voice glorify the God and Father of our Lord Jesus Christ. . . .

May the God of hope fill you with all joy and peace in believing, so that by the power of the Holy Spirit you may abound in hope. (Rom. 15:5–6, 13)

May the God of peace be with you all. Amen. (Rom. 15:33)

The grace of the Lord Jesus Christ and the love of God and the fellowship of the Holy Spirit be with you all. (2 Cor. 13:14)

Peace be to the brothers, and love with faith, from God the Father and the Lord Jesus Christ. Grace be with all who love our Lord Jesus Christ with love incorruptible. (Eph. 6:23–24)

Now may our Lord Jesus Christ himself, and God our Father, who loved us and gave us eternal comfort and good hope through grace, comfort your hearts and establish them in every good work and word. (2 Thess. 2:16–17)

But the Lord is faithful. He will establish you and guard you against the evil one. And we have confidence in the Lord about you, that you are doing and will do the things that we command. May the Lord direct your hearts to the love of God and to the steadfastness of Christ. (2 Thess. 3:3–5)

Now may the Lord of peace himself give you peace at all times in every way. The Lord be with you all. (2 Thess. 3:16)

Now may the God of peace who brought again from the dead our Lord Jesus, the great shepherd of the sheep, by the blood of the eternal covenant, equip you with everything good that you

> may do his will, working in us that which is pleasing in his sight, through Jesus Christ, to whom be glory forever and ever. Amen. (Heb. 13:20–21)

A benediction is more than a mere prayer—it is an impartation. It pronounces God's name and nourishing grace over others. Through benedictions, we place God's name and his blessing upon his people. We see this in the Aaronic Blessing, which may be the most familiar benediction of all time.

> The LORD spoke to Moses, saying, "Speak to Aaron and his sons, saying, Thus you shall bless the people of Israel: you shall say to them,
>
> The LORD bless you and keep you;
> the LORD make his face to shine upon you and be gracious to you;
> the LORD lift up his countenance upon you and give you peace.
>
> "So shall they put my name upon the people of Israel, and I will bless them." (Num. 6:22–27)

Notice that in the case of Aaron's benediction, God makes the promise that, through the benediction, he *will* bless the people. The blessing is secured because a benediction is prayed. When prayed sincerely, benedictions are prayers for blessings that God honors and answers. This would explain the confidence Paul has in the benediction that he himself prays in 1 Thessalonians 5:23–24:

> Now may the God of peace himself sanctify you completely, and may your whole spirit and soul and body be kept blameless at the coming of our Lord Jesus Christ. He who calls you is faithful; he will surely do it.

When I say to you in faith, "May God bless you and give you grace and peace," he will. For he who has called you will be faithful to do it.

SAYING "HI" AND "BYE" IN NOURISHING STYLE

Paul started and ended nearly all his letters with a benediction—with some variation of "Grace be to you" or "Grace be with you." One could say that benedictions and blessings are a Christian way to say "Hi" and "Bye" in highly nourishing style. At minimum, such words set a tone and direction for each time that we meet and part in our relationships. When benedictions start and finish conversations, they establish an intentional goal for what happens in between. They say, "I come to impart peace and grace to you, and I want to leave you with peace and grace. And may it be that everything I say or do between my 'hi' and 'bye' infuses your heart with more peace and grace than you had when we met."

I am not advocating for a wooden repetition of words. "Empty phrases" (or *vain repetitions,* as the old King James Version puts it) are of no value (Matt. 6:7). What we need is a conscious relational commitment to edify and nourish others. And this commitment could well be helped along by actual words of blessing: "May the Lord give you peace." "Peace be upon you and yours." "Grace be to you, and grace, peace, and joy go with you." Speaking these words as we greet one another and say our farewells will go a long way toward creating a new climate of grace and goodwill together.

If such grace-filled sentiments are sincerely in our hearts (even if not on our lips) whenever we greet one another and say goodbye, they will affect the tone and trajectory of all our conversations. After all, it becomes far more difficult—or at least it should—to curse someone whom we really and truly want to bless (see James 3:8–10). Such spiritual double-mindedness will still occur, but not nearly as often. When our intent for every conversation we have is to bless and nourish, better things are bound to happen.

GOD AND THE GOSPEL

I have often counseled young preachers to make sure that in every sermon they preach, no matter its text or topic, they give people more of God and the gospel. People need the whole Word of God, but they also need to see God and the gospel wherever they turn in that Word. Life is too hard and sins are too many for us to take our eyes off God or leave our hearts disconnected from the gospel of his saving and forgiving grace.

And you may need that gospel right now. I hope you have been excited by the themes of this chapter—for that has been my goal in writing it. But along with that excitement, you may also have felt a measure of conviction as you've assessed the nourishing quality of your words. I have. While I have rejoiced over these truths, I've also had to pause a few times in order to massage a deepening ache in my heart. While thinking about the positive nourishing good that words are supposed to provide, I have wondered how many of my own words have failed in that purpose. God has made me sensitive to these matters for many years, but I still sin all too often. If nourishing grace and edifying strength are to be the aim of all my conversations, then I've wasted too many of those conversations. Quite possibly, you have become aware of the same truth about yourself.

How many times have our verbal Hurricane Sandys blown through and uprooted trust, grace, and love, or otherwise damaged the relationships we are called to build? And how many times has our goal been to win arguments, or to make our point, or to show off our knowledge, or to just get the conversation over with so that we can move on as quickly as possible to far more pleasant things?

Sources say that the average person speaks around fifteen thousand words per day. Considering the large family I am a part of, as well as the counseling, preaching, teaching, phone calls, office interactions, and witnessing to my neighbors that I am involved with, I am sure that I reach twenty-five thousand per day—especially if I include all the words that I *type* day in and day out. That's about 383,250,000 words so far in my adult life—which is more than enough to make a man tremble. How many thousands of times—in either preaching or counseling or casual conversation—have my words failed to nourish? How many times have they wounded instead? Does it make you wonder? Whatever your own word count, these questions are worth asking.

You and I both need to find hope in the mercy of God through Jesus and to express it in confession and prayer. As I've reflected on my less-than-nourishing speech, the following prayer has come to my mind. Feel free to eavesdrop as I offer it to the Lord. And if you need to pause and pray a similar prayer, then by all means do so. It may do your soul—and your relationships—some good.

> Jesus, my lips and heart are stained with too much sin. Please forgive me for my every unkind and destructive word—and for all the nourishing words that I could have and should have spoken, but never did. I know you have heard all my hurtful words and have wept when I've spoken them. I know too that you've observed all the opportunities I've missed to speak what would have edified and nourished and have wept over those as well. I am so sorry, dear Savior; for I have sinned. When I have failed to yield to your Spirit's control, I have had an unkind and unloving tongue. Thank you, Lord Jesus, for dying for my sinful lips. Thank you for washing my mouth—not with soap, but with mercy and grace. Thank you for coming so willingly to pay my debt and cancel all my hurtful words. Thank you for grace, grace, grace—costly to you, but free for me.

Jesus, you paid it all.
All to you I owe.
Sin had left a crimson stain.
You washed it white as snow.[3]

Now please, O Lord, help me to see the power and potential of my words—to know that you give me countless opportunities every day to be a blessing with my words! Inspire me to make grace, mercy, and peace the guiding motivations for all that I say. Give me the grace to do and speak better things. Even as I dare to ask for your pardon from sin, I also ask for your power to change and for you to anoint my words. I pray for all this through the merits of Jesus's atoning blood and perfect righteousness alone. Amen.

And now, may I pray for you?

The Lord bless you and keep you;
The Lord make his face to shine upon you and be gracious to you;
The Lord lift up his countenance upon you
And give you peace.
In Jesus's Name, amen.

DISCUSSION AND REFLECTION

1. Did reading this chapter cause you any grief as you reflected on the nourishing quality of your own words (or their lack thereof)? What steps could you take to share your grief with others and ask them to pray that you would have grace to change?

3. Adapted from Elvina M. Hall, "Jesus Paid It All," 1865.

2. "The gladness of relationships is nourished by your grace-filled lips" suggests that there is a direct connection between how nourishing our words are and how glad or joyful our relationships will be. Describe an experience in which someone's nourishing words filled you with joy. Then describe a time when your nourishing words did that for someone else.
3. How did the collection of benedictions and blessings in this chapter affect you? Do you think any good would come from replacing "hi" and "bye" with blessings—even just simple blessings?
4. How did you do on the Psalm 19 Test? Which of the questions most affected your conscience?
5. If you speak fifteen thousand words per day, what percentage of them would you say are nourishing? Would your closest family and friends agree?

CHILL

OPEN UP

MAKE TIME

MEAN WHAT YOU SAY

UNDERSTAND WHAT YOU HEAR

NOURISH WITH GRACE

INITIATE PEACE

CELEBRATE OTHERS

ASSUME YOU ARE WRONG

THINK THE BEST

EXAMINE YOUR HEART

7

INITIATE PEACE

"If possible, so far as it depends on you, live peaceably with all." (Rom. 12:18)

"Be angry and do not sin; do not let the sun go down on your anger, and give no opportunity to the devil." (Eph. 4:26–27)

To make the peace you wish you had,
Don't ever go to bed still mad!

The most hair-raising experience I've had with any of God's creatures occurred in the twenty-second year of my life. I was a young college grad awaiting my first ministry assignment and working in the meantime as a maintenance guy at an apartment complex. One day my boss ordered me to grab a pesticide tank and head to building 4, apartment 6, in order to deal with an infestation of cockroaches. By then an experienced roach hunter, I wasn't surprised to be called to lead the charge. But little did I know the scale of the conflict that would ensue.

Building 4, apartment 6 belonged to a hoarder. The tenant threw away nothing. The only way through her apartment was an eighteen-inch path between mountains of clothes, newspapers, books, paper bags, and clutter that covered the floor, which branched off to lead to each room. Such clutter is a great disadvantage in roach hunting. It is a roach haven—a refuge into which innumerable roaches can flee and hide.

I began my assault by raiding the dark places where roaches gather. Wherever I sprayed—under sinks, behind refrigerators, beside stoves, inside cupboards—thousands of roaches swarmed over every surface. The kitchen counter backsplash was a fake-brick plastic wall covering; as I peeled it off, the sudden light sent many thousands more roaches scurrying in all directions like a massive, disoriented mini-orc army. I sprayed the vermin dead—but my tank quickly ran dry. Though it carried enough bug poison to kill thousands of roaches, there were still far more roaches alive than dead by the time it was empty.

This was skin-crawling work, but it had to be done. After arming myself with several roach bombs, I returned and set them off in the small, two-bedroom apartment. The next day I returned yet again to assess the carnage. Tens of thousands of dead roaches littered every surface throughout the apartment.

Let me reiterate that someone actually lived in that apartment. She had for years—and she moved back in following the Great Roach War, despite my doubts that we'd gotten all the roaches. There were too many dark places for the vermin to lay low until the air cleared—the occupant had created the conditions for a long-term roach conflict. There had once been a day when that apartment was 100-percent roach free. But not now—and probably, without the intervention of a Pentagon-issue bomb, not ever again.

How had this happened? One thing is for sure: those pests didn't march into building 4, apartment 6, as a creepy, crawly, million-bug army from Mordor. My best guess is that the first roach occupiers were an innocent, domestic-minded newlywed couple that thought apartment 6 would be a nice place to settle. Pick a cozy spot. Clear some under-the-sink space. Settle in and settle down. Have kids. Build a nice life for themselves.

That's why, when the war was over, I checked each piece of my clothing with a careful eye, lest I inadvertently carry the enemy home to start an infestation in the apartment where Gayline and I lived. When I removed my Converse high-tops and saw a single solitary surviving roach crawling out of my left sneaker, I made sure that his vain attempt at escape ended quickly and decisively. I was not going to let my place become his starter home into which he could bring a new bride. Not. On. My. Watch.

My friend, roach plagues don't begin a million strong. Roaches come in ones and twos. An infestation starts small . . . and, for that matter, so do bitter divorces, family feuds, church splits, racial hostilities, and international conflicts.

ALL ABOUT A HOG

You've probably heard of the famous Hatfield-McCoy feud. Back in the 1800s, these two neighboring families turned their region into a thirty-year war zone as they engaged in one of the United States' bloodiest family feuds. Fierce hatred. Legal warfare. Family betrayals. Brutal beatings. Around a dozen murders. At least eight life imprisonments. One death by execution. All this resulted from the feud.

And, according to multiple reports, this bitter dispute started when one family accused the other of stealing a hog. It was all about a single solitary pig. People committed sordid deeds and awful crimes—all over a bit of bacon. Look, I love bacon as much as the next guy; but if only some good-hearted peacemaker had said, "You know what? The bacon isn't worth it." If only.

MATERNAL WRATH AND SIBLING ISSUES

Go back over four thousand years ago to 2000 BC. After a long wait, Abraham had two sons—but by two women: Ishmael (by his servant Hagar) and Isaac (by his wife Sarah). Their relationship was doomed from the start, due to their father's (singular) and mothers' (plural) dysfunctional family life (see Gen. 16:1–16). Their mothers' jealousy of each other led to serious sibling issues, which were foretold in Genesis 16:11–12. These were fueled further in in Genesis 21:8–21, when Ishmael did what big brothers do: he teased the little guy (see vv. 9–10).

From that point on, the two were destined to be at odds. Isaac was a patriarch over Israel and Ishmael over what would become the Arab world. And there you have it. The intractable millennia-long Arab-Israeli conflict in the Middle East is complicated, and there is plenty of guilt to share all around—but at least in part, it traces back to some domestic jealousy and sibling trash talk. God had his sovereign plan for all this; but still, it's too bad that somebody didn't have the foresight to step in and make peace way back when Ishmael got some kicks out of teasing his little brother. If only.

LIKE FATHER, LIKE CHILDREN

The story of the prodigal son in Luke 15:11–32 is much more about a father's eager peacemaking forgiveness than it is about a son's prodigal behavior. And, as you may well know, it is ultimately about our heavenly Father's eager peacemaking love and forgiveness. It is a story about the Father above who waits for his children to repent and return home. It is about the One who stands and looks into the distance in order to catch the first glimpse of the repenting prodigal's return home—and into the orbit of his love and peace.

God is a God who is "ready to forgive"—in other words, he is a God of forgiveness—"gracious and merciful, slow to anger and abounding in steadfast love" (Neh. 9:17). He is a God whose very nature and impulse is to forgive and make peace. He is neither slow nor hesitant to forgive. He has made peace through the blood of his Son (see Eph. 2:13–18), and he applies that peace to us as soon as we ask for it in faith (see Rom. 5:1).

So it is that as Jesus establishes the basic ground rules for the kingdom of God—which are known as the *Beatitudes*—he identifies peacemakers as "sons of God" (Matt. 5:9). To be called a *son of God* is to be recognized as one who bears a family likeness to God—one who reflects the image and nature of the One who loves and makes peace with us. According to Jesus, being a peacemaker wins a person the honor of being a proverbial apple that doesn't fall far from the divine Tree.

Peacemaking is both a function and consequence of communication. Initiating peace requires both speaking and hearing words. James, having already rebuked cursing, jealousy, boasting, and all other war-inciting communication sins, calls us to the wisdom that is "from above"—that wisdom that is "first pure, then *peaceable*, gentle, open to reason, full of mercy and good fruits, impartial and sincere" (James 3:14–17). Then he reminds us that "a harvest of righteousness is sown in peace by those who make peace" (v. 18). We need to initiate peace, through our communication, if we want to gather in a harvest of righteousness.

THE *WHO* AND *WHEN* OF PEACEMAKING

Since good and thorough books about peacemaking have already been written, I will not duplicate their work here.[1] What I want us to see here is the importance of *who* initiates the peace process and *when* it is to happen. The answer to the *who* question is "me." The answer to the *when* question is "now."

I am the *who*—the one who is to seek peace. This is clear from our Lord's own words in Matthew's gospel. When it comes to reconciling with others and seeking peace, it makes no difference whether I am the offender or the offended. The offended is charged to seek reconciliation in Matthew 18:15: "If your brother *sins against you,* go and tell him his fault, between you and him

1. See for example, Ken Sande, *The Peacemaker: A Biblical Guide to Resolving Personal Conflict,* 3rd ed. (Grand Rapids: Baker Books, 2004).

alone. If he listens to you, you have gained your brother." In Matthew 5:23–24, the offender is similarly charged.

> So if you are offering your gift at the altar and there remember that *your brother has something against you,* leave your gift there before the altar and go. First be reconciled to your brother, and then come and offer your gift.

In the first passage, the burden of responsibility is placed on the one who has been sinned against; in the second, the guilty party is required to initiate peace.

In other words, according to Jesus, the responsibility to take initiative in peacemaking is always *mine.*[2] The call to initiate peace is one that no one can ignore. If I am sinned against by others, I must go and seek peace. And if I have *sinned* against others, I must do the same.[3] I am called to initiate peace wherever, whenever, and with whomever I can.

As for the *when* of peacemaking, the time is *now*. Jesus taught us that if a conflict comes to our minds while we are offering

2. Biblical peace (which is also known as *shalom*) is a state of healing and wholeness in all of life. It is when physical, emotional, spiritual, and relational well-being exists—when things are as they should be. Jesus's point is that when such wholeness does not exist in our relationships, it is our responsibility to pursue it to the best of our ability. For a warm, pastoral look at shalom and biblical peace in its varied expressions, see Andy Farmer, *Real Peace: What We Long for and Where to Find It* (Wheaton, IL: Crossway, 2013).

3. It needs to be said that making peace does not include excusing or enabling criminal or abusive behavior in the name of grace or forgiveness. In the case of criminal behavior or physical or sexual abuse, victim-survivors need to seek and secure safety—both for themselves and for other potential victims. This requires the prosecution and punishment of any who are guilty in such cases (see Rom. 13:1–4). The call to make peace does not take precedence over the punishment of wrongdoers and the protection of the innocent through the civil authorities God has established.

This isn't to suggest that it is right or healthy for victim-survivors to harbor rage or hatred, but it is to say that justice and safety are essential.

worship to God, we should leave our worship half-finished in order to go and make peace. Paul reaffirms this as well:

> Be angry and do not sin; do not let the sun go down on your anger, and give no opportunity to the devil. (Eph. 4:26–27)

While these words have been understood in various ways, I believe Paul means that we must resolve never to go to bed mad.[4] To the best of our ability, we need to resolve anger and restore shalom in our relationships—something that's as close to relational wholeness as is possible—before bedtime.[5] This is a call to active and aggressive peacemaking. Peace is, in the first place, a matter of the heart—I need to *want* it. It is then a matter of the clock—I need to want it before bedtime.

> To make the peace you wish you had,
> Don't ever go to bed still mad!

This is possible. And what's more, it works.

4. I take this view for four reasons. First, in the context of these verses, Paul is talking about being angry with people—not being angry at sin, as some have suggested. Second, a call to short-term anger seems to be the most natural meaning of Paul's words, since elsewhere in Ephesians 4 he has called us to maintain a "bond of peace" (v. 3), to put away bitterness, which is the result of festering, unresolved anger (see v. 31), and to offer kind, tenderhearted forgiveness (see v. 32). Third, the psalm that Paul is quoting in these verses commands believers to be silent when they go to bed, in response to which the psalmist asserts that he will sleep in *peace* (see Ps. 4:4, 8). Finally, the reason that Paul gives for not letting the sun go down on our wrath is so that we will not give the devil an opportunity. To my mind, it makes the most sense that he is warning us that prolonged anger is the opening that the devil uses to come in and destroy our relationships.

5. Strictly speaking, shalom, as noted above, is about more than the absence of conflict. It is a state of well-being and wholeness in every part of life, and relationships are one area in which it finds expression. Tim Keller defines it as "complete reconciliation, a state of the fullest flourishing in every dimension—physical, emotional, social, and spiritual—because all relationships

Bill and Betty were a sweet couple in their seventies who came to love Jesus deeply. But common grace—the vestige of God's image—was evident in them both even before their faith matured. They enjoyed a long and happy marriage that traced back to the "before Christ" era of their lives. When this dear couple celebrated their fiftieth anniversary, I asked them for the secret of their marriage success. They responded simultaneously with an answer that revealed a conscious and deliberate commitment that they both shared: "We never went to bed mad." They made peace every day.

This is one secret to relational longevity. Never go to bed mad. Do everything in your power, every day, to let your heart and your relationships sleep in peace. Gayline and I are more than forty years in, and—by the grace of God—we can echo Bill and Betty's testimony. This is not a boast; it's a fact. By the ever-present help of the Holy Spirit, we have never gone to bed mad. The fact that this hothead can say such a thing bears witness to the astonishing, transforming grace of God—grace that is as available to you as it is to me.

ESCALATION: THE WAY THAT ANGER WORKS

There is a reason we are exhorted to make peace so urgently. Paul says that when we allow our anger to continue into tomorrow, we give the devil an "opportunity" (Eph. 4:27). As Yusufu Turaki explains, "Anger is sometimes justified, but brooding on anger and being preoccupied by it is sinful. It can easily provide a foothold for the devil to use to promote evil. That is why it should not be allowed to linger overnight."[6] Satan's opportunity is not

---

are right, perfect, and filled with joy." See Timothy Keller, *Generous Justice: How God's Care Makes Us Just* (New York: Penguin Books, 2016), 173–74.

6. Yusufu Turaki, "Ephesians," in *Africa Bible Commentary: A One-Volume Commentary Written by 70 African Scholars*, ed. Tokunboh Adeyemo, 2nd ed. (Grand Rapids: Zondervan Academic, 2010), 1461.

anger so much as it is *unresolved* anger. It is in the very nature of anger to escalate—and Satan uses this escalation to divide the church, conquer it, and wreak havoc in it.

Notice the escalation that Matthew 5:25–26 portrays:

> Come to terms quickly with your accuser while you are going with him to court, lest your accuser hand you over to the judge, and the judge to the guard, and you be put in prison. Truly, I say to you, you will never get out until you have paid the last penny.

If peace is not made now, then somebody—at least metaphorically—is going to land in court, before a judge, under guard, and finally in a jail.

Things get worse if we don't make them better. "The beginning of strife is like letting out water, so quit before the quarrel breaks out" (Prov. 17:14). Initiate peace—and do it now. And if the other party isn't ready for peace, then make sure that you always are. Be poised. Ready. Willing. Eager.

MY HEART HAS BEEN HARDENING

Just this past Sunday, Rosalynn, a dear sister in Christ, asked my forgiveness because she had been "hardening her heart" against me. In her cultural heritage, she is used to pastors addressing the personal trials of their churches' members on Sundays, along with any societal turmoil that took place during the week, and offering comfort and hope to their flocks in the context of specific ongoing hardships. For brothers and sisters from that heritage, congregational worship is also about congregational lament and healing. My culture is different—and less biblical in this regard. People like me don't do lament and healing well. Unless there is a massive national or international crisis that is felt by all, I have seldom processed weekly news by lamenting or felt much need to address current cultural traumas from the pulpit. But to those who are accustomed to this—and who, with good reason, feel the need for it—my silence comes across as indifference.

So what did Rosalynn do with her hurt? She became a peacemaker. She initiated conversation with me in order to ask my forgiveness. She could feel her heart hardening against me, and she came to me in peace and humble grace. She didn't let the hurt fester. Blessed is this peacemaker! Because of her love, I was able to ask for *her* forgiveness, express my sorrow, and embrace my sister. Further, because of her reconciling efforts, she, her husband, and I are getting together this week to talk. Understanding and love will prevail—all because she initiated peace without delay. She shall be called a daughter of God!

YOU CAN ONLY DO YOU

When it comes to peace, you cannot make other people's choices. You can only do you. So Paul's instruction to us is both helpful and realistic when he says, "If possible, so far as it depends on you, live peaceably with all" (Rom. 12:18). Do what you can do, and say what you can say. Then wait in hope and prayer.

If you're finding it almost impossibly hard to pursue peace, then may I recommend that you examine your heart? Check out your inner person and see what's ruling it. If you are more interested in nursing a grudge, or winning an argument, or proving yourself right, or exacting your pound of flesh, or squaring the score than you are in honoring Christ and nourishing others with grace, then you've got a bigger problem than your little squabble with Neighbor Ned. You've got major heart surgery to do—an *idol-ectomy* to perform.

But if what matters most to you is that Christ be pleased and that his image in others be nourished and loved in peace, then take the Romans 12 road that is provided below, and good things will happen.

A PEACE PRIMER FROM ROMANS 12

I often recommend Romans 12:9–21 as a go-to guide for peacemakers everywhere. In fact, it's a good *peace primer* to read prayerfully whenever you find yourself feeling angry with others and needing to embark on a peacemaking or peacekeeping mission.

- Pray a lot (v. 12).
- Look to honor the image, not to belittle or despise it (v. 10).
- Seek to bless, not to curse (v. 14).
- Understand, sympathize, and empathize (v. 15).
- Be humbly ready to learn (v. 16).
- Clothe all your words and deeds with kindness (vv. 13, 20–21).
- Relinquish the "need" to win, get even, or enforce justice (vv. 17, 19)
- Choose forgiving harmony over angry discord (v. 16).
- Affirm that you are genuinely *for* one another in love (vv. 9–10).
- Pray again (v. 12).

THE RELATIONSHIP-HEALING EFFECTS OF COMMUNION

In his kindness, our Lord Jesus Christ has woven a sacrament right into the fabric of each faithful church that both motivates us and helps us to seek peace. It is the communion meal. Similarly to how Jesus tells us to be reconciled to one another before we offer sacrifices to God, Paul argues in 1 Corinthians 11 that we should do the same when we approach the Lord's Supper. He argues that conscientious participation in the Communion meal will make for peace.

Here's how it works. In the Lord's Supper, the body of Christ (i.e., the church) truly shares the body of Christ (meaning his very real spiritual presence, which is symbolized through the Communion elements). We are in fellowship with one another as we fellowship with Jesus through his holy supper (see 1 Cor. 10:16–17). It is this vertical *and* horizontal fellowship that take place during Communion that should make us careful about how we participate in it. That is what Paul addresses in 1 Corinthians 11:17–34. If we are peace-breakers who allow "divisions" in the church (v. 18), or if we let people go hungry (see v. 21), or if we despise and humiliate others by degrading them on the basis of class and culture distinctions (see v. 22; see also 10:31–32), we turn the Lord's Supper into a non-supper and negate its value in our lives (see 11:17–20).

For this reason, Paul admonishes us to examine ourselves in order to get our hearts and relationships right *before* we participate in the meal, lest we eat and drink the Father's discipline onto ourselves (11:27–32). This makes the Lord's Supper a great blessing to our relationships. It turns the approaching meal into a much-needed cue for us to check our relationships and make sure they are all as they should be before we eat or drink. The rhythm of regular Communion observance gives us a recurring reminder and imperative to make peace. Calvin the Reformer says that Communion compels us to think about how our actions have grieved others for whom Christ died—others who share the same loaf and cup with us—and to repent.[7] It is for this very reason that Augustine called the Communion sacrament a "bond of charity," or love.[8]

7. See I. John Hesselink, *Calvin's First Catechism: A Commentary* (Louisville: Westminster John Knox Press, 1998), 152.

8. The early church father extolled Communion with these rapturous words: "Would you then also live by the Spirit of Christ. Be in the body of

Seeing Communion as a bond of love and peace goes a long way toward helping us to keep short accounts of our anger, jealousy, and bitterness toward each other in the church. It compels us to make peace before our next time around the Table. However often you and your church observe Communion, I recommend that you turn your preparation for it into a peacemaking season.

NOW, ABOUT THAT PARKING SPACE

Having a peaceable disposition is a decision, and the time to decide is now, before the flood breaks. A couple of years back, I noticed over the course of several days that my parking space, directly in front of my home, was being filled by someone else. In this urban suburb, that's a no-no. Whoever this insensitive clod was, I was not pleased. With each new day, my resentment of him increased, even though he was as yet an unidentified culprit.

I made up my mind to find out who the parking-space bandit was and why he was taking my spot. Praying hard that I would have a good attitude in the process—which I was very much tempted *not* to have—I came to suspect one neighbor, and because I didn't want the stolen parking spot to be a bone of contention between him and me, I knocked on his door while praying that the Lord would give me grace to come in peace.

Joe answered, and in a moment or two it was clear that he *was* the culprit, but that he also had good reason to be parked in my spot. His own normal space around the corner had been commandeered by a road crew. He apologized quickly, rendering the

---

Christ. . . . It is for this that the Apostle Paul expounding this bread, says: *'One bread,'* says he, *'we being many are one body.'* 1 Corinthians 10:17. O mystery of piety! O sign of unity! O bond of charity! He that would live has where to live, has whence to live. Let him draw near, let him believe: let him be embodied, that he may be made to live. Let him not shrink from the compact of members; let him not be a rotten member that deserves to be cut off; let him not be a deformed member whereof to be ashamed; let him be a fair,

parking issue moot in about thirty seconds—and proving himself not to be an insensitive clod after all. I then seized the moment to introduce myself as his neighbor from two doors down, mentioning that I was a pastor of a new church in town.

He jumped on that, saying that God had been giving him a strong kick in the pants. A recent stroke had awakened him to a fresh awareness of God and had stirred him to read the New Testament. "I haven't got down on my knees and invited God in yet, but he's knocking, and I'm reading," he said.

I shared the grace of God with him—grace that is offered through the death and righteousness of Jesus—and he listened closely. Then he added, "I'm thinking that God may have had something to do with that roadwork and my car being in front of your house." Yeah; I think so, Joe. Since then, we've become good friends who have hung out on multiple occasions. And, oh—by the way, all the indicators are that Joe is now a brother in the Lord. He has professed faith and demonstrated a hunger and commitment to follow Jesus. Imagine my joy when just yesterday he closed out a message to me with the words "Yours in Christ." How glad I am that the Lord gave me that grace to seek peace early rather than too late!

And it's a funny thing—this week has been *déjà vu*. Someone else's car has been sitting snugly in my spot for days. Once again I've been in slow-to-a-boil mode. In fact, I just looked out my window *again* to see if I could catch a glimpse of the culprit. There he is! I'm looking at him right now. He's a twentysomething guy scraping snow off his car—*the* car. At Gayline's urging, I realize that *now* is the time to do this again. Excuse me as I get up and go to ensure peace with my new neighbor.

---

fit, and sound member; let him cleave to the body." Augustine, tractate 26 of "Homilies on the Gospel of John," trans. John Gibb and James Innes, in *Augustin: Gospel of John, First Epistle of John, Soliloquies*, Nicene and Post-Nicene Fathers, ed. Philip Schaff, 1st ser., vol. 7 (repr., Peabody, MA: Hendrickson Publications, 2004), 172.

Here's hoping that I behave like a peacemaking apple that stays close to the Tree.

FIVE MINUTES LATER

I'm back. And I've got the start of a new friendship. Anger is gone. Understanding now reigns. Peace prevails. Satan loses. And God is up to something once again. This peacemaking thing is a sure path to joy.

Is there a conflict or situation that needs your own peacemaking attention right now, before you move on to chapter 8? Remember that "a harvest of righteousness is sown in peace by those who make peace" (James 3:18).

DISCUSSION AND REFLECTION

1. "To make the peace you wish you had, don't ever go to bed still mad" is a good rule of thumb—but it is not always easy. Describe a time when you tried to make peace quickly. How did it work out?
2. Have you ever experienced the escalation of anger that happens when peace is not made quickly? Would it have been easier for you in that situation if you'd made peace on day one?
3. When you hear spouses describe having a commitment to never go to bed mad, how do you respond? Does such a commitment seem unrealistic?
4. If Communion is meant to be a cue for us to make peace, how will you approach the Lord's Supper differently from now on? If you are a spiritual leader, in your home or the church, what are ways in which you can help others to do this more consistently?
5. Do you have any ongoing conflicts that need a peaceful resolution? How will you begin to take the path toward peace?

CHILL

OPEN UP

MAKE TIME

MEAN WHAT YOU SAY

UNDERSTAND WHAT YOU HEAR

NOURISH WITH GRACE

INITIATE PEACE

CELEBRATE OTHERS

ASSUME YOU ARE WRONG

THINK THE BEST

EXAMINE YOUR HEART

8

CELEBRATE OTHERS

"Well done, good and faithful servant." (Matt. 25:21)

"Each one will receive his commendation from God." (1 Cor. 4:5)

Take moments with each human being
To celebrate the grace you're seeing.

I never knew him personally, but from everything I have read, the man was a complete enigma. As a matter of religious discipline, he observed a careful diet, never took a drop of alcohol, and complied with an odd ritual vow that had been imposed on him at birth. That was about it as far as the virtues he had—at least as far as any human eye could see. Dwarfing this list was a moral rap sheet that was longer than a Puritan sermon. Things started imploding early on when he defied his parents' wisdom and counsel. After that, without their guidance or a functioning moral compass of his own, he was lost and confused for the duration of his life.

He showed an astonishing level of naivete (or was it raging lust?) when it came to women. He consorted with prostitutes, and the two women he had recorded relationships with were so culturally and religiously ill-fitted for him that only defiant rebellion, or blind lust, or adolescent immaturity can account for his choices. In the end, one betrayed him for her family and the other for money. His second lover, whose betrayal led to his untimely death, functioned as a mole who was planted by his enemies to uncover the secret to his personal and military exploits. The records indicate that he killed a lot of bad people in his day. But there is little to no hint that he ever did so for any noble purpose. If you're grasping for a visual, don't envision Captain America or the Black Panther. Think of a guy with a white-hot temper that fueled a fierce thirst for enemy blood.

The man died as an ancient type of suicide bomber—or more like a suicide bomb. After being captured and blinded by his enemies, he was chained one day between two massive pillars, which supported a large house that held three thousand of his enemies partying on the roof above and many more inside. With sudden superhuman strength that was imparted by God—who considered the three thousand to be his enemies, too—the man snapped those pillars and brought down the house with his bare hands, killing his foes along with himself. Notably, there is no sign that the man was acting out of any true zeal for God's honor. Even in this final act, he seemed to be only—as he always had been—about himself.

The man's name was Samson. You can read his story, in gory detail, in Judges 13–16.

HEAVEN'S HALL OF FAITH

So where would you place Samson on your list of role models? You wouldn't place him anywhere—and neither would I. But God has. Hebrews 11 has been famously called the "Hall of Faith" chapter of the Bible. It begins and ends with divine commendations of the faith of various Old Testament figures. It opens with the words "For by [faith] the people of old received their commendation" (v. 2) and then proceeds to name about twenty men and women of faith (and to reference dozens more)—all of whom were "commended through their faith" (v. 39).

There is a precious truth tucked away in Hebrews 11. The word *commend* is a translation of a Greek word that is elsewhere translated as *witness* or *bear witness*. This *commendation* that these biblical figures receive is a favorable testimony—a kind of heavenly vote of confidence. In other words, God steps forward as a character witness to vouch for these men and women. But his doing so is more than a formal commendation; he is also displaying personal, heartfelt approval. Early in the chapter, we are taught that a faith that believes that God exists, and that he rewards the type of faith that we see in all these Old Testament figures, *pleases* God (see v. 6). It brings joy to his heart.

God goes so far as to say that these were all men and women "of whom the world was not worthy" (v. 38). *Worthy* is a word involving scales and weights. When weighed on the scale of worth by God, the world is a featherweight compared to these believers. Just as Jesus is worthier than Moses (see Heb. 3:3), these old-covenant believers were worthier than the rest of humanity. They had value in God's eyes that the world was unfit even to behold. As far as he is concerned, the human race didn't deserve to have these people walking among them.

Because these men and women belonged to and looked for another, better world (see Heb. 11:10, 13–16, 35), they became people of greater substance and worth. And in this chapter of Hebrews, God makes sure to tell us how he feels about them. Might we almost say that he is proud of them—much as he seemed to be of another ancient believer: Job (see Job 1:8; 2:3)?

One is tempted to ask whether this is for real, considering the people who are in view. Does God *really* render such high praise of, and proudly celebrate, *these* people? Read the captions that Hebrews attaches to each of these Hall of Faith honorees, and you will see their varying acts of faith. What you will *not* see are their glaring sins. This is the reverse of today's world. Today's social and mainstream media aggrandize celebrities and leaders one minute and then demonize them the next. Character assassination—especially (but not exclusively) against people with whom we disagree—is the blood sport of our generation. Vicious *diss*-course sells more ad space than does respectful discourse. We love to pedestal people and then chop them down inch by inch—one brutal post or tweet at a time.

Imagine what our culture's mob-like lust to destroy people would do with the men and women of faith we see in Hebrews 11. The social and mainstream-media frenzy over them would be vicious. Abraham, for instance, twice doubted his safety and put his wife's honor at risk in order to save his own skin (see Gen. 12:10–20; 20:1–13). Sarah doubted God's promises, essentially laughing in his face (see Gen. 18:9–15). Isaac doubted, just as his dad had, and pulled the same dishonest, wife-risking tricks in order to try to keep himself alive (see Gen. 26:6–11). Jacob was a conniving con artist who wouldn't stop until God literally wrestled him into faith and submission (see Gen. 25:29–34; 27–32). Joseph was an indiscreet—if not arrogant—younger brother whose unwise reports of how God favored him over his brothers led to prolonged trials (see Gen. 37:1–28). Moses was a murderer-turned-deliverer who never got into the promised land because he took matters into his own hands (see Ex. 2:11–12; Num. 20:2–13; Deut. 3:23–27). The people of Israel crossed the Red Sea by faith but then died in the wilderness because of their unbelief (see Num. 14:1–35). Rahab, the woman who helped Israel achieve its first major conquest in the promised land, was a harlot (see Josh. 2:1–21). Gideon was a hesitant doubter who later became, as did many Old Testament believers, a confirmed polygamist (see Judg. 6:11–22; 8:29–30). Barak was anything but a man's man (see Judg. 4:4–9). Jephthah lacked common sense and fatherly decency (see Judg. 11:29–40). David was an adulterer and a murderer (see 2 Sam. 11). Samuel was a flawed father (see 1 Sam. 8:1–3). And Samson was Samson.

Yet there isn't a word of any of this in Hebrews 11. Even though nearly every man or woman who is named in Hebrews could also be cited for significant moral failure and doubt, none are. Not here. Not now. Hebrews 11 is not about failure; it's about faith. It is not about condemnation; it's about commendation. It is not about public censure; it's about heavenly praise. There is a place for divine correction and even discipline—and each of these men and women received it in due time. But at heart, God cannot resist faith when he sees it. It pleases him so deeply that it inspires his happy and holy praise.

WHAT DID GOD SEE?

So what did God see in Samson? He saw what none of us would have seen: a heart of faith. Reread the Judges 13–16 account, making sure to read between the lines, and you will see that, for all his many and egregious sins, Samson really and truly *believed*. Deep inside his twisted and confused self, he knew where to turn for help when he needed it (see Judg. 15:18; 16:28). He knew that the source of his strength was God and that without God's help he was no stronger than any other person was (see Judg. 16:17).

None of this condones Samson's sins, which were scandalous and costly. But they were not the full story of Samson's life—nor would they define his status before God. This is because God sees and celebrates what we too often fail to see, and he overlooks that upon which we tend to fixate. When he assesses a life, he measures it with an eye for what is good. As Christopher Love wrote in his old Puritanese,

> Weak Christians look more on their sins than on their graces; yet God looks on their graces and overlooks their sins and infirmities. The Holy Ghost said, "Ye have heard of the patience of Job." He might also have said, "Ye have heard of the impatience

> of Job," but God reckons His people not by what is bad in them, but by what is good in them. Mention is made of Rahab's [protection] of the spies, but no mention is made that she told a lie when she did so. That which was well done was mentioned to her praise, and what was amiss, is buried in silence, or, at least, is not recorded against her and charged upon her. . . . O it is good serving such a master, who is ready to reward the good we do, and is ready to forgive and pass by what is amiss. Therefore, you who have but little grace, yet remember that God will have His eye on that little grace. He will not quench the smoking flax, nor break the bruised reed.[1]

This is God's amazing, praising grace.

A PRAISING GOD

We will soon arrive at our communication principle; but before we do, let's be sure to let what we have seen affect how we think and feel. God's delight in his children, and his commitment to praise them, can be seen so pervasively throughout the Word that one is tempted to come right out and say it with joy: the Father is really proud of his kids—and he wants us to know it.

Every time the Father promises them a future reward, it's a reminder that he loves to honor his children. What are the words "Well done, good and faithful servant. You have been faithful over a little; I will set you over much. Enter into the joy of your master" (Matt. 25:21; see also Luke 19:17), if not a promise that Jesus is going to celebrate the faithful good we have done in this life? How do we understand the words "Each one will receive his commendation from God" (1 Cor. 4:5), if not as a promise that

1. Christopher Love, sermon on 2 Timothy 2 (preached at St. Lawrence Jewry, London, April 20, 1651), quoted in Don Kistler, *Why Read the Puritans Today?* (Orlando: Soli Deo Gloria, 1999).

the Day is coming when the Father will praise us for the lives we have lived? Likewise, when we read that those who are inwardly circumcised (that is, consecrated to God) will receive praise from God (see Rom. 2:29), how can we not dare to hope? What can be the possible meaning of Romans 2:6–10, which assures us that for "those who by patience in well-doing seek for glory and honor . . . *there will be* . . . glory and honor," if not that God is going to honor us? And how are we to respond when Peter tells us that after our faith is tested and proven by passing through the fire, it will "result in praise and glory and honor at the revelation of Jesus Christ" (1 Peter 1:7)? It's easy to miss that Peter is writing about *our* praise, honor, and glory—which Jesus will give to us when he is revealed.

You might respond that we do not deserve any of this—and you would be right. We deserve only hell. By the strict equation of merit, we would not earn any praise. But because of God's standard of mercy, he will give it to us anyway. Or you may rightly say that we will cast our crowns before King Jesus in heaven in order to deflect glory from ourselves to him—the only really worthy one whom there is (see Rev. 4:10–11). You might also affirm that it is through the righteousness and power of Christ alone that all our works will endure the test of the Day that is to come and will gain their reward. And you would most assuredly be right. For, after all, anything good in us—including the faith we have that pleases God—is a gift of God in the first place (see Eph. 2:8; Phil. 1:29).

But let us not miss the truth that the crowns that we cast at his feet will be *our* crowns that we will have worn on *our* heads when we sit on *our* thrones in order to rule over cities and towns that are placed under *our* authority in a new earth that is being prepared as *our* eternal home, where *our* faces and forms will shine forever like the noonday sun (see Prov. 4:18; Dan. 12:3; Matt. 13:43). In the Father's eyes, this present world is not worthy of *us*, either. This is stunning. Certainly it is not what I see when I look in the mirror or glance across the church aisle. But that only goes to show that God sees and celebrates very differently from the way we do.

DO UNTO OTHERS WHAT WILL BE DONE UNTO YOU

I have lingered on God's celebration of us for two reasons. First, I want the wonder of God's amazing, praising grace to fill us with joyful anticipation—which I hope it has done. Second, I want the wonder of God's amazing, praising grace to set the standard for how we look at and treat one another. The promise that God is going to praise us is a call for us to do unto others what will be done unto us. If this is how God celebrates us in love, and if I am to imitate his love and live as his image, then this is how I should see and celebrate others.

Paul knew this to be true. In virtually all his letters, he expressed joy and gratitude for the wonderful grace that was so evident in his readers' lives. He called the Philippians his joy and crown (see Phil. 4:1). He even commended unbelievers for the common grace that he saw in their lives (see Acts 17:22; 22:3; 24:15; 26:27).

I suspect he took lessons from his early mentor and friend, Barnabas, who was nicknamed "son of encouragement" (Acts 4:36) because he had an uncommon ability to see and affirm the grace of God in people's lives. He could see what others couldn't. He did this with the new believers in Antioch (see Acts 11:22–24); he did it on Paul's behalf (Acts 9:26–27); and he did it with John Mark, in whom he saw grace and potential that Paul could see only later (see Acts 15:36–39; 2 Tim. 4:11). Together, Paul and Barnabas are New Testament examples of a celebratory life. They model Golden-Rule love in action—the skill of seeing grace and celebrating it.

A MUTUAL CELEBRATION SOCIETY

In the movie *The Greatest Showman*, P. T. Barnum gathers all kinds of people together who do not fit the mold. Called freaks by many, these unique human beings find their place in a new family. The real-life Barnum may have had dubious motives behind all this, but however much the movie may whitewash his bio line, it produces a memorable scene in which this band of unwanteds sing about their dignity, refusing to be reduced to "dust" and claiming to be "glorious."[2] It is a stirring moment in which humanity, in all its shapes and sizes, is celebrated.

Biblically-minded Christians will feel a tension here. Even now, I find myself grasping for the right balance in the way I think about human beings. The Bible teaches the reality of both human dignity (which is to be honored) and human depravity (which is to be mourned), and it's hard to express these truths together in the proper proportion. Too many in the world focus exclusively on the first. Too many in the church focus too much on the second.

Nowadays, humans are proud and proud of it; we have become a mutual admiration society that boasts about everything that we are—including our sin. Given how much God hates pride (see Prov. 6:16–17; 8:13; 16:5), this is a massive problem. Secular humanism is an issue. It is a sin to celebrate human actions or lifestyles that defy divine law. It is blasphemy to claim that humans are glorious while denying that God is infinitely more glorious. Man's smug satisfaction with man is idolatry.

Meanwhile, many in the church have so emphasized the depravity of man that they have lost sight of the wonder of what it means to be human—wonder that God has bestowed. With a

2. See chapter 13 of *The Greatest Showman*, directed by Michael Gracey (2017; Beverly Hills, CA: Twentieth Century Fox Home Entertainment, 2018), DVD.

narrow focus on sin, they have created a distorted view that fails to see the wonder of what theologians call *common grace*—grace that is common to all—or to appreciate human dignity and even accomplishment.

There is a way for us to hold these two truths in balance. We can guard against implicit godless humanism by remembering that we are made by an all-powerful Creator—in his image but also out of dust. We can avoid vain self-confidence by realizing that it is in God alone that "we live and move and have our being" (Acts 17:28). We can guard against the all-too-common temptation of self-worship by believing that "from him and through him and to him are all things" and thus that he alone is worthy of glory forever (Rom. 11:36). And we can avoid arrogant self-righteousness by refusing to live in denial of our deep depravity.

But if pride is a perversion of human dignity, so is the profanity[3] of belittlement. Be-*little*-ment trivializes, marginalizes, ostracizes, or demonizes people who bear the majestic and glorious image (see Ps. 8:4–5) and are destined for glory (see Rom. 2:6–10). When the eternal Day dawns, all of redeemed humanity will be robed with immortality and will dazzle with a glory that outshines the noonday sun. Heaven will be an eternal mutual *celebration* society in which we will cheer all that we have become by the creating and transforming grace of God.

STOP THE DISS-COURSE

This is good reason for us to start clearing some clutter now—to get rid of all put-downs and *diss*-course and to replace them

3. I believe that Christians need to develop a broader and deeper understanding of the nature of profanity. Profanity is not merely the use of crude four-letter words. It happens any time we treat someone or something that is wonderful, extraordinary, clean, magnificent, or terrifyingly holy as if it were common, ordinary, unclean, or trivial (see Appendix B: A Word about Profanity).

with verbal affirmations and respect. Name-calling, insults, wrath, slander, and malice are not fitting for those who "have put on the new self, which is being renewed in knowledge after the image of its creator" (Col. 3:10; see also vv. 8–9). And they do not honor others who have also been made in that image (remember James 3:9–10). We must forsake the caustic and hateful speech that is winning the day in both the world and the church. Those who bear the image are not to be cussed at or mocked. There should be no cutting sarcasm, no belittling, no dissing, no rants, no demonizing. As Paul puts it, we must stop biting and devouring one another, lest we be consumed by each other (see Gal. 5:15).

But avoiding put-downs alone does not reprogram our hearts to sync with the heart of God. God calls us to *celebrate* others—as he celebrates us. He wants us to create a climate of encouragement and positive, affirming, celebratory respect in all our relationships at all times.

> Take moments with each human being
> To celebrate the grace you're seeing.

As the Word says, "Love one another with brotherly affection. Outdo one another in showing honor" (Rom. 12:10) and "Pay to all what is owed to them: . . . respect to whom respect is owed, honor to whom honor is owed" (Rom. 13:7). To paraphrase Philippians 2:3, in humility let us esteem and elevate others as being higher than and superior to ourselves. Let us see each and *every* other (with no exceptions) in this way, and then let us speak accordingly. By doing this, we will turn conversations into celebrations.

FLATTERY AND THE PARADOX OF PRAISE

You may worry that I am advocating flattery. But in terms of both its nature and its fruits, affirmation is very different from flattery. Flattery is a lie; affirmation is the truth (see Prov. 28:23). Flattery says what isn't true, and it does so out of a selfish ulterior motive (see Prov. 29:5). Biblical encouragement speaks celebratory truth, and it does so in order to edify. Flattery whispers how "good" we are, in order to seduce us to do evil. Affirmation calls attention to the goodness that God has produced within us, in order to inspire us to be even better. Flattery tells unbelievers that everything is okay. Encouragement tells unbelievers where they are right, but not right enough (see Acts 17:22–23; 22:3; 26:27). Flattery is devil-like (see Gen 3:4–5); affirmation, as we have seen, is godlike.

You may also worry that affirmation will tempt people to be prideful. But it's a paradox of praise that the opposite is often true: sincere believers are often humbled when they are praised. Since they know that any good in them is by God's grace alone, praise reminds them of how underserving they are and how worthy God is.

It is when we do *not* experience appreciation that we are most tempted to be prideful. When I receive praise, I feel like I don't deserve it; when I don't receive praise, I feel like I do deserve it. Humility grows in a regenerated, newborn heart when praise is given. Pride grows when it is withheld. That's the paradox. Affirm a believer's value, and he will want to give glory to God. Ignore or diminish that value, and he will grasp for all the glory he can get. Withhold praise, and others will crave it. Render praise, and they will cast crowns at the Savior's feet with grateful joy. Such is the mystery of grace.

BECOMING FLUENT IN CELEBRATION

If you are not well-practiced in celebration, you may find that fluency in the language of encouragement doesn't come easily. I learned this biblical grace thirty years into my adult life, which meant that for thirty years I had been doing relationships wrong.

I had to pray hard for grace and discipline to enable me just to *consider* others, so that I could then honor them as my equals and superiors.

I also had to learn how to *speak* what I saw. Encouragement can't happen unless we actually encourage. As my friend Andrew Kalvelege—a world-class encourager in his own right—once said to me, "If you don't communicate it, it doesn't count." Celebratory relationships don't *go without saying*. They require that we become fluent in authentic affirmation.

DEVELOPING CELEBRATION FLUENCY

Here are some suggestions to help you to improve your fluency in the grace of celebration.

- Look for the image of God in others—any sign of creativity, skill, dignity, or courage.
- Look for natural abilities that they have cultivated through hard work and effort.
- Look for faith in God that has persevered under trial.
- Look for the fruit of the Spirit: love, joy, peace, patience, kindness, goodness, faithfulness, gentleness, and self-control (Gal. 5:22–23).
- Look for the gifts of the Spirit: Spirit-prompted and empowered abilities that others are using to serve (Rom. 12:6–8; 1 Cor. 12:28).
- Look for character growth in specific areas.
- Look for service and kindness that you can praise.
- Look for positive influence that others are having in their church, the world, and their families.

Look for qualities you can celebrate in all your daily relationships, and then make sure to say what you see. Otherwise it doesn't count.

CULTURAL CELEBRATION

There is another application of celebration that transcends our individual relationships. Recently I went with some dear friends to an almost entirely African-American event. This was my first experience observing uninhibited friendship and fellowship among black believers in Jesus. As those who were normally in the minority became the majority, my black brothers and sisters were free to be themselves, unfiltered and unaltered—to release colloquialisms, tones, emotions, laughter, mannerisms, and love in ways that reflected fully and freely the cultural heritage of which they are a part. The cultural style and expression were so different from my own that my friends asked me later whether it made me uncomfortable. Quite the opposite—it was fantastic! I felt a powerful joy from this immersive experience in a culture that was not my own—a culture that was brimming with beauty, energy, lament, and joy.

When we expand the affirmation and respect that we show to others beyond the boundaries of our individual relationships and seek to pursue cross-cultural appreciation as well, we will encourage a mutually enhancing celebration of diversity in the church. The more we and the people who are like us commit to getting as close as we can to those who are from other cultures in order to see and appreciate how they live, love, display faith, and worship Christ, the more we will celebrate the almost infinite nuances within our human family, the more fully human we will feel ourselves to be, and the more God's multicultural vision for the church will come to pass (see Eph. 3:6–11).

Mutual celebration will lead to mutual flourishing—in all our individual and collective relationships. What Tony Evans says about the church is true across the terrain of every human connection that we have. "A kingdom perspective urges us to open our eyes, hearts, and minds in order to take what we learn about ourselves, and from each other, with regard to the strengths inherent within each of us, and merge these together to form a more productive union. . . . If the church can ever merge strength with strength in order to create a more complete whole, there will be no stopping the impact we can have not only in our nation, but in our world."[4]

Dr. Soong-Chan Rah agrees. "When we are dealing with cross-cultural and multicultural ministry, it is important to see God at work in all cultures, not just one. . . . A healthy interaction between two disparate [i.e., different] cultures [or genders, generations, and/or socio-economic conditions] can challenge those from each to bring out the best in both [or all]."[5]

I commend this vision as a way of life. For if we fail to receive and believe this vision, we will suffer the ill effects of our narrow perspectives and will lose our chance to flourish in our friendships, our homes, our churches, and the world. But when we make much of God by celebrating those who bear his image, we ourselves will be blessed and beautified. The end result is that all of us will experience larger hearts and increased grace.

DISCUSSION AND REFLECTION

1. If you are to "take moments with each human being to celebrate the grace you're seeing," then what specific people do you think you should start with?
2. Are you a celebrator of people? Do your words more often put people down or build people up? What would others say about you in this area?

4. Tony Evans, *Oneness Embraced: Reconciliation, the Kingdom, and How We Are Stronger Together* (Chicago, IL: Moody Publishers, 2011), 18–19.

5. Soong-Chan Rah, *Many Colors: Cultural Intelligence for a Changing World* (Chicago: Moody Publishers, 2010) 18, 100.

3. Recheck the list of suggestions for developing your celebration fluency. Pick one of them to put into practice, with at least one person, at some point during the next twenty-four hours. When you have done so, describe what the experience was like. How did the person respond? How did you feel in the process?
4. "If you don't communicate it, it doesn't count." Do you ever observe positive things in others but fail to tell them about it? Why do you think that is?
5. Have you ever been in a cross-cultural setting in which you were part of a tiny minority? What was it like? What did you enjoy about it? What was hard about it? If you are in the majority, have you ever wondered what those who are always in the minority must feel when their culture is muted by a more dominant one?

CHILL

OPEN UP

MAKE TIME

MEAN WHAT YOU SAY

UNDERSTAND WHAT YOU HEAR

NOURISH WITH GRACE

INITIATE PEACE

CELEBRATE OTHERS

ASSUME YOU ARE WRONG

THINK THE BEST

EXAMINE YOUR HEART

9

ASSUME YOU ARE WRONG

"Do you see a man who is wise in his own eyes?
There is more hope for a fool than for him." (Prov. 26:12)

"'Knowledge' puffs up, but love builds up. If anyone imagines that he knows something, he does not yet know as he ought to know." (1 Cor. 8:1–2)

That you are wrong you may assume—
And by this give the truth some room.

A while ago a Christian bookseller friend of mine got into a pretty intense squabble with a customer who had called to complain vehemently. The dispute was over a set of books that the customer had ordered—this irate book-buyer was complaining that he had not received all twenty-three volumes.

The man's hostile tone revealed obvious failure-to-chill issues. Worse was the striking resemblance that he bore to a cantankerous mule. Even when my friend told him that there were only twenty-*two* volumes in the set, and that all twenty-two had been sent to him, his wrath continued unabated. Against all the facts, he kept pressing his argument—unwilling to concede his error.

Eventually he ended the phone call by threatening my friend, his Christian brother, with a lawsuit.

Let me venture a guess that the buyer was a Calvinist (of the sixteenth-century variety). After all, the set of books that was in dispute was a twenty-two-volume set of Calvin's commentaries on the Bible—not exactly a hot-ticket item for non-Calvinist types. Besides, the man knew how to fight without backing down—something for which we Calvinists are all too well known. I've seen enough headstrong, ornery Calvinists in my time—and have been one of them myself—to lead me to assume that our lawsuit-threatening theological thug might well have been numbered among them himself. But, in keeping with this chapter's point, *I could be wrong*.

COMIC OR TRAGIC?

Here's the irony: in his unappeasable, lawsuit-wielding wrath, this irate theologian, Calvinist or otherwise, violated the teaching of the Bible (see 1 Cor. 6:1–8) in order to acquire teaching about the Bible. He did the unholy even as he tried to learn more about the holy. We all do this. We dispute, we quarrel, we grow angry, we impugn motives, we start yelling and accusing, we dig in our heels—and all in haughty defense of things we believe to be true and pure and right and good. Alexander Strauch writes, "In many church disputes, believers fight for so-called truths that are not explicitly revealed in Scripture while egregiously violating the clear and repeated teaching of Scripture on godly conduct and attitudes."[1] Just as people do who introduce their thoughts with the phrase "With all due respect" and then proceed without any respect at all, many people feign good intentions as they bite and devour another. It would be comic if it weren't so tragic.

1. Alexander Strauch, *If You Bite and Devour One Another* (Littleton, CO: Lewis and Roth, 2011), 18.

You may not be a theological mule in particular, but it's a good bet that you are mulish about *something*. It may be politics, or education options, or family finances, or what restaurant to go to, or what really happened last Tuesday, or whether or not good Christians may ever drink alcohol or watch TV or read Harry Potter or cheer for the Patriots. It's a good bet—although I'm not a gambling man—that within thirty seconds you could think of at least three debatable topics about which you *know* you are right and on which no one could get you to back down.

ASSUME YOU ARE WRONG

We need to curb our mulishness by learning how to coexist humbly, peacefully, and teachably with one another—even when we disagree. Part of the secret to doing this is to assume what is counterintuitive: that in every disagreement, we may very well be wrong.

> That you are wrong you may assume—
> And by this give the truth some room.

The assumption that our opinions and perspectives are wrong is *so* counterintuitive that more than one person has argued that I'm wrong on this point. "After all," they reason, "if I think or 'know' that I'm right, then why would I assume that I'm wrong? Where is the logic in that?"

In order to answer these questions, let us first consider what this principle means. When I say to assume you are *wrong,* I mean *wrong* in at least some way—whether it's on the basis of opinion, or attitude, or word choice, or emphasis, or tone, or grasp of the relevant information, or timing. We should enter every conversation—and especially every dispute—with a confidence that there will be something for us to learn, something for us to confess, something that we did not know as we ought to have known it or need to know it. That I am not all-knowing should be more than a statement of the obvious; it should be a conscious, functioning conviction that humbles me all the time.

Consistently practicing the self-awareness that tells us we may be at least partly wrong saves us from a lot of grief and angry *diss*-course. After all, if we assume that we're wrong, then we don't have to be right. And if we don't have to be right, then we don't have to fight. As Wayne Dyer has asked, "Did you ever notice how difficult it is to argue with someone who's not obsessed with being right?"[2] Yes. It is almost impossible. Assuming that we are wrong, and not needing to be right, are game changers that impact our communication and our relationships with dramatic effect.

SEARCHING THE SCRIPTURES

But is this self-doubt biblical? In my pretty dogmatic opinion, it most emphatically is! True humility assumes that I am in error—at least in part.

> The way of a fool is right in his own eyes,
> but a wise man listens to advice. (Prov. 12:15)

> Do you see a man who is wise in his own eyes?
> There is more hope for a fool than for him. (Prov. 26:12)

> Never be wise in your own sight. (Rom. 12:16)

Fools have no self-doubt. The wise know that they need more wisdom. If I am in a dispute with you, taking a realistic approach

2. Wayne W. Dyer, quoted in Robin R. Laysears-Smith, *Thoughts That Feed the Resilient Mind: Affirmations to Stay Resilient* (Bloomington, IN: Balboa Press, 2013), 37.

will lead me to assume the presence of ignorance—not in you but in *me*.

Claims that we know things for certain—especially if they are matters that Scripture doesn't address or is less clear about than others—are symptomatic of pride. Correcting the Corinthians about their conflicts over disputable matters, Paul wrote, "'Knowledge' puffs up, but love builds up. If anyone imagines that he knows something, he does not yet know as he ought to know" (1 Cor. 8:1–2). Likewise, the wisdom that is "from above" is "open to reason" (James 3:17). This means that those who have heavenly wisdom can be persuaded, which means that they are teachable, which means that they know they have to learn, which means that they assume they are at least partly wrong.

Readers will know that we cannot be like God in this area, since he is always right and never wrong. But theologically speaking, assuming that we are wrong is a function of biblical anthropology. What the Bible says about human nature in general reinforces the texts above. As creatures, we are limited beings who do not know everything. There's a difference between being made in the image of God and *being* God. God is omniscient; he never has to be taught anything, because he already knows everything (see Isa. 40:13–14; Rom. 11:33–34). Man is ignorant; he can know and remember only whatever God chooses to reveal to him and store up in him. Combine our creatureliness with our sinfulness, and we have every reason to doubt our own understanding. We know very little, and what we do know is clouded and distorted by our sinful selves.

This leads the humble person to say, "I am aware that I do not and cannot know all the facts. I am also conscious that I can never know another person's intentions or all the factors that led him to do what he did or say what he said. Further, I am sure that I am at least partly wrong regarding my interpretation of Scripture, or of other people's intentions, or of any actions or circumstances that are relevant to this dispute. And yes—since I am a sinner, to boot,

I am going to function in this disagreement as if I really believe all this and sincerely assume that I am wrong."

THE AGE ADVANTAGE

The longer we live—as long as we have an ounce of sense—the more we know that we do not know. It's the age advantage that young folks just don't have. I once heard a man quip, "A teenager is someone who knows not—but knows not that he knows not." Older people are not so unaware—unless they're just plain fools (King Solomon's term, not mine). If they have learned anything in life, it's that they don't know much of anything at all.

Knowing the folly of youth, Gayline and I established a rule in our home. Nobody in our family—not any of our six children nor either of their parents—was allowed to say, "I know" to begin an assertion of anything other than the clear, inarguable, primary truths of God's Word. Every other perspective or opinion had to be set up with words like "I think" or "I may be wrong" or "I don't know enough to be sure." We didn't apply this perfectly, but it was our consistent way of training our children (and ourselves) to assume a measure of error in all our thoughts.

Part of wise humility is not only knowing that you do not know but making sure others know that you know it as well. We make a transformative difference in our relationships when we cultivate the habit of using humble words. Such words, which create what we might call a vocabulary of self-doubt, show that we do not need to be right and send a clear signal that we are not gunning for a fight.

VOCABULARY OF SELF-DOUBT

Here are some phrases and questions that exude heavenly wisdom when we say them and mean them.

- I think . . .
- I may be wrong, but it seems . . .
- I don't have all the info, but my sense (which could be wrong) is . . .
- I can't offer a dogmatic opinion, since I don't know enough facts yet.
- I just don't know.
- This is only a perception, but is it okay if I share that . . .
- You know more about this than I do.
- Can you help me to understand?
- I'm seeing things differently; can you help me see what am I missing?

A RIGHT TO MY OPINION?

Given how impulsively, assertively, and stubbornly people argue for their points of view, they clearly believe the mantra that "everybody's entitled to their opinion." But are we so entitled? The short answer is: on a few things, yes; on most things, probably not. And, whether we are entitled to them or not, we should temper our opinions on *any* topic with the humility of self-doubt and the grace of being conscious about our fallibility.

There are a few things about which we may—and must—possess an assured confidence: those truths that are indisputably revealed by God in Scripture (for example, the Trinity, the deity, the atonement, the resurrection, the reign and return of Jesus, justification by grace alone through faith alone because of Christ alone) and other such matters as might be found, for example, in the Apostles' Creed when it is biblically understood. These things we *know*, because God has made them known.

However, we should adjust the strength of our opinions on

most things. This is not to say that there are no important things besides the ones above; it's simply to say that the further we move from the center—from the things about which God has spoken unambiguously—the more we should hold our convictions with a humble willingness to learn. We will all define this center with slight variations, and that's okay. But let's have the grace to recognize that there *is* a center, which is of first importance (see 1 Cor. 15:3–5) and which we are to hold with blood-earnest conviction. Then let us also recognize that there is an off-center and periphery, which is of lesser importance or certainty and which we are to hold with a strong sense that the things we know are probably far fewer than the things we *don't* know.

Our right to our own opinion—whether about biblical matters, or about economic or foreign policy, or about the guilt or innocence of the latest public figure to be accused of sin, or about "white privilege," or about "black culture," or about why people vote Republican or Democrat (or Conservative, Labour, or Green Party), or about who said what three weeks ago, or about who should take the garbage out—is contingent upon how clear and confirmed the evidence is and how thoroughly we have studied the issues and the opinions surrounding them. If we don't study and understand the evidence, we have little right to our own opinion on it. When we give an opinion that is uninformed, we add nothing but ignorance to the conversation.

Let me say this with sure and certain knowledge: Tim Shorey has no right to an opinion about how to best treat cancer or erase our national deficit or solve the Middle East crisis or apply quantum physics. And if truth be faced, unless I have given many hours of study and reflection to a host of other matters, I probably shouldn't have any opinions about any of them, either—at least not dogmatic opinions. The less I know about a subject, the less confident I should be in my opinion concerning it. In all things, we should cultivate the good, healthy self-doubt of conscious fallibility.

Dr. Rah suggests that each disagreement has the potential to be either a "battle of messages" or "a learning conversation." In a *battle of messages,* I aim to prove my point and persuade you that I am right. In a *learning conversation,* I assume that there are important things I do not know. "In a battle of messages, we fight over who gets to be right," while "a learning conversation places a higher value on learning than scoring points and proving yourself correct."[3] Consider the change that getting this right would make in the tone, intensity, and frequency of our conflicts. But the humility that is necessary for assuming that we are wrong and that we have something to learn will not be gained easily.

THE ALLURE OF THE LAST WORD

Few things prove our lust to be right and our desperation *not* to be wrong more than the allure of the *last word.* Even as a veteran believer for many years, I still have to put a stranglehold on my tongue to keep it from saying "Just one more thing" when a conflict is winding down.

This battle is neither rare nor new. Centuries ago, Pastor John Newton wrote, "I believe scarcely any thing has [contributed] so much to perpetuate disputes and dissensions in the professing church as the ambition [to have] the last word."[4] Just when an argument is about to flame out, someone's "one more thing" fuels the fight for another day. An insistence on getting the last opinion in, and an inability to let something go without the closure of being proven right, ignites the blaze afresh.

Paul had to deal with such tendencies in his day, too. With respect to disputable matters, he said, "[Do] not . . . quarrel over opinions. . . . Why do you pass judgment on your brother? Or you,

3. Soong-Chan Rah, *Many Colors: Cultural Intelligence for a Changing World* (Chicago: Moody Publishers, 2010), 133; see also 132–36.

4. Grant Gordon, ed., *Wise Counsel: John Newton's Letters to John Ryland Jr.* (Carlisle, PA: Banner of Truth Trust, 2009) 251.

why do you despise your brother? For we will all stand before the judgment seat of God. . . . Each of us will give an account of himself to God" (Rom. 14:1, 10, 12). In other words, let it go. Only God gets the last word.

And if this is true of our disagreements over such significant matters as religious holy days and other issues of conscience (which is what the dispute in Romans 14 was about), then how much more is it true for all the minor disagreements that we have in everyday life? If I know that God has the final say, then I do not need to clinch victory with a buzzer-beater last word or achieve closure with my "one more thing to add."

Each one of us answers to God and will be held accountable for every perspective he or she has ever had. With that in mind, we can and should have whatever respectful and humble conversations we need to have so that we can understand one another—and then leave one another alone with his or her opinion.[5]

OWNING OUR 2 PERCENT

Given our fallibility and sin, we should hold our perceptions and opinions loosely and expect to be wrong. And if, on rare occasions, we end up being wrong about being wrong, we should be as amazed that we got it right as everyone else is—and should render praise to God, where it belongs.[6]

5. It is important that the humility of self-doubt reign even when opinions vary between leaders and followers. Those who lead must practice the grace of *conscious fallibility* before, during, and after decisions are made. Leaders and followers alike should (1) pray for agreement, (2) seek outside counsel, (3) apply all the COMMUNICATE principles diligently, and (4) express to one another their awareness that they may be wrong. For a wonderful expression of such mutual humility, see James B. Hurley, *Man and Woman in Biblical Perspective* (Grand Rapids: Zondervan, 2002), 150–52.

6. "[God] has graciously accommodated Himself to my weakness, borne with my mistakes, and helped me through innumerable prejudices, which, but for His mercy, would have been insuperable hindrances! I have therefore no

Nevertheless, even when our opinions may be right, we will likely still own some blame in every dispute. Someone once told me that we should always ask, "Are there ways I can take personal responsibility for at least some part of this conflict?" And then he added, "Even if I am only 2 percent responsible for a conflict, I am 100 percent responsible for that 2 percent!"

This good counsel calls for what I once heard described as "impossible humility": humility that is so hard, so demanding, so selfless, that it seems too lofty an ideal to hold. But it isn't really impossible—only miraculous. It is a humble self-knowledge that is inspired and enabled by God and that produces in us an awareness that we are fallible in every way—a self-doubt that changes our primary goal when we disagree with someone. Through this grace of teachable humility, we gain a new ambition. Instead of needing to prove our point, we aim only to *im*prove our hearts, our minds, and our relationships.

TWO BARRIERS TO SELF-DOUBT

If we are going to develop a healthy self-doubt, we will need to surmount two barriers. The first is *isolation*. When we live in a world of isolated decisions, ideas, and cultures, we tend to develop fixed opinions on many topics. Since the only ideas and perspectives we ever hear in this case are our own or those of others just like us, we never stand corrected. Trillia Newbell cites this as one benefit of living in a city with many different people. "Cities force individuals to refine their cultural assumptions, religious beliefs, and sense of calling as they run up against the sharp edges of the assumptions, beliefs, and expertise of other city dwellers."[7]

---

right to be angry, impatient, or censorious to others, especially as I have still much to learn." John Newton to Mrs. Thornton, November 1775, in *Letters of John Newton* (Carlisle, PA: Banner of Truth Trust, 2007), 274.

7. Trillia J. Newbell, *United: Captured by God's Vision for Diversity* (Chicago: Moody, 2014), 130.

There are applications of this for our homes, our churches, our friends, and our enemies as well. Mix with old and young, male and female, black and white and brown, rich and poor, and all the combinations that these categories produce, and you *will* learn healthy self-doubt. Widen your conversations and diversify your dialogue within the body of Christ. Doing so will sharpen your faith, test your assumptions, reveal your errors, enlighten your understanding of the Bible, clarify the truth, and help you grow in a way that is gospel centered, driven by the Word, and nurtured by your relationships. These great blessings can be ours when we assume that we are wrong and choose to "run up against the sharp edges" of others' perspectives.

If isolation is one barrier to our developing a healthy self-doubt, *power* is another. Our willingness to assume that we are wrong is often imperiled by the temptations we experience when we are in a stronger—and allegedly superior—position. Whoever has authority or majority status tends to assume a *superiority* status as well, which can further lead them to assume an infallibility status. Learning conversations—to use Dr. Rah's phrase—are hard for people who are in power or positions of authority. Be careful of this, whoever you are and whatever your position—whether you are a husband, parent, teacher, or pastor. I know the perils of power well, since in every role and position I occupy that include advantage, authority, or power—such as my roles as father, husband, pastor, and white male—I have at times assumed myself to be right when I was very wrong.

Power and advantage are a part of life, and few—if any—of us are spared their temptation or peril. We have all probably assumed ourselves to be right in at least one relationship in which we have held authority or the status of power. Dads and moms do it. Rich people do it. The more educated do it to the less educated. Older siblings do it to younger siblings. Nations do it to other nations. Cultures do it to other cultures. Whoever has the advantage of being in power or in the majority tends to assume that their opinions are superior.

Such power advantages need to be neutralized by humility. I am not arguing that we should undermine God's ordained leadership roles in the home and the church in favor of an egalitarian equality. That is not God's design. But it is his design that everyone—including those who are in positions of influence and authority—recognize their great need for the insight and input of those whom they lead and love. This has to happen both spontaneously and in structured ways. We need to assume that we are wrong and act like we mean it. We then need to create means—whether in our homes, the church, or the world—by which various voices can receive a hearing. If we assume that we are wrong, we will not only listen carefully when others speak but will create more ways for them to speak.

HOW THE GOSPEL FREES YOU TO BE FEARLESSLY WRONG

This kind of humility requires a very real vulnerability. We feel unsafe when we admit that we may be wrong, and we fear that others may think less of us or may take advantage of us. And if we admit that we actually *are* wrong, there's no telling what others will do with that. Some of us find our identity in always being right. Our self-image is based on an illusion of infallibility. We find security in the delusion that we have all the answers. And because we crave this false security, we don't dare admit the possibility of being wrong.

There are others of us, however, who seem to have an excessive measure of self-doubt. We may be inclined to think we are wrong all the time and in every way. Perhaps we have been on the receiving end of oppressive dogmatic leadership that has beaten down our opinions for so long that we now assume we are never right at all. When we are in a place of excessive self-doubt, it can be very hard for us to share any ideas, lest we be "wrong" yet again—or *assumed* to be wrong by those around us.

Whichever of these two temptations we are prone to, we all need some gospel help in this area. At the heart of the gospel is the promise that, even though we are sinners who are often wrong, we are treated as if we have never done wrong and have always been right(eous). Christ's imputed righteousness justifies us before God (see Rom. 3:23–26; 5:18–21; Titus 3:4–7) and positions us so that even if we are accused or guilty, we cannot be charged or condemned (see Rom. 5:1; 8:1, 31–34).

Who can condemn those whom God has justified? Who can charge those to whom God has given his amnesty? If the highest Judge in the universe has declared us to be right, then no one who would accuse or damn us can make their charges stick. There is no higher court of appeal. If he who has never done any wrong was willing to be treated as wrong so that we might be counted as right, then what can any sinful man or minion of hell say about it? My friend, this is the good news. It is a deep well of courage and a shield of faith. The good news of our unchangeable standing in the grace of God frees us from both the pride of assuming that we are always right and from the paralysis of thinking that we never are. It enables us to be open to other views and to openly share our own. It secures us in Christ so that we can assume that we have both something to learn and something to say—and that if we are wrong in the process, it's all going to be all right.

Imagine how it would alter the climate of our homes, enrich the air quality of our marriages, restore the wholeness of our churches, improve the health of our pastoral teams, and enhance our multicolored and multicultured human experiences if all of us, secure in the love of Christ and the forever justifying verdict of God, began to assume that we might well be wrong but also a bit right—and then grew from there.

DISCUSSION AND REFLECTION

1. "That you are wrong you may assume—and by this give the truth some room" is a good rule of thumb. Can you identify a relationship in which you need to adjust your assumptions and seek to learn where you are wrong?
2. Are there any conflicts in your life in which you are 2 percent wrong? If so, what do you think you should do with that 2 percent of the blame that is yours?
3. What are you "mulish" about? Can you identify an opinion or perspective that you hold with dogmatic certainty but which is not in fact a known certainty? How should you rethink your certainty about it?
4. Does the desire to have the "last word" affect you? Describe a time when your "last word" comment *extended* an argument instead of ended it. What would you do differently if you were able to live out that argument again?
5. What would it mean to combine gospel security with self-doubt? What difference might it make if you had such a combination in your life and relationships?

CHILL

OPEN UP

MAKE TIME

MEAN WHAT YOU SAY

UNDERSTAND WHAT YOU HEAR

NOURISH WITH GRACE

INITIATE PEACE

CELEBRATE OTHERS

ASSUME YOU ARE WRONG

THINK THE BEST

EXAMINE YOUR HEART

10

THINK THE BEST

"Love bears all things, believes all things, hopes all things, endures all things." (1 Cor. 13:7)

"But if [the land] bears thorns and thistles, it is worthless and near to being cursed, and its end is to be burned. Though we speak in this way, yet in your case, beloved, we feel sure of better things—things that belong to salvation." (Heb. 6:8–9)

Before you jump to think the worst,
Believe the best—judge kindly first.

If you have never left a child behind, you are a better parent than I. Maybe it's because six kids are hard to keep track of; maybe it's because finiteness oozes out my pores; maybe it's because I'm a bad dad. Whatever the cause, I've done it at least three times; and each time proved to be traumatic—quite possibly for the kids, too.

David's turn came when he was five. One Saturday morning around 7:15, I was studying in my home office when Gayline said some quick early-morning goodbyes. She was taking the children to an event that had long been on the calendar and was leaving me in a quiet house. After she left, I awaited the arrival of a couple of guys I was mentoring. However, just before 7:30, one called to ask whether he could pick me up to meet the other at a restaurant instead. I agreed. He came. We went. We ate. We talked. We had a great time.

I was in blissful pastoral mode—oblivious until I hopped back in the car and started the fifteen-minute ride home. Suddenly, the alert flashed across my mind: "David's home alone!" I had forgotten that Gayline had taken just the older kids, not the youngest. David had been left asleep in bed. So I grabbed my friend's car phone—back when they were the thing—and called home in order to connect to my poor child. As the phone rang, I prayed that no one would answer. Perhaps he was still asleep. My heart sank when he answered after a couple of rings—quiet and timid, but surprisingly not in anguished distress.

Begging his forgiveness, I told him that I was on my way home. I held him on the line the whole way, talking with him about anything and everything, so that he would feel my verbal presence. When we arrived, I jumped out of the car, raced toward the door, threw it open, and rushed inside to swoop him up into my arms. If it had been a scene from *Little House on the Prairie*—for those who are old enough to remember—everything would have gone into slow motion, with heart-stirring music playing dramatically as two long-separated family members ran into each other's arms.

Actually, I was the only one running. David was casual and calm. I was guilt- and grief-stricken and apologized profusely through tears. "It's my fault, David. I am so sorry. Please forgive me. It's my fault," I said time and again to comfort him. His simple, sincere, tearless response was "It's okay, Dad. It's okay. It's okay, Dad. It's okay." He said that time and again to comfort me.

Later that day, as I shared the experience with friends—confessing my parenting blunder and still grieving my failure—David interrupted our adult conversation with words that I will never forget: "Dad kept saying he was sorry and that it was his fault. But I like to think that it was no one's fault." Just like that, our five-year-old offered me the grace of charitable judgment. He thought the best. While it still very much was my fault, he discerned between intentional wrongdoing and accidental mistake—and drew a merciful conclusion.

And I started crying all over again.

THE BEST POSSIBLE LIGHT

David gave me a loving benefit of the doubt by putting the best possible interpretation on my actions. He did for me what we grown-ups all too often fail to do for one another. Too often our relationships crash and burn at the intersection where an offending action and a hypercritical, uncharitable interpretive reaction meet.

Here is the premise of this chapter. Since God alone knows the thoughts and intentions of the heart, he alone can judge what people are really thinking and why they *really* do the things that they do. It is not our prerogative to judge people's motives and actions badly. Instead, we are to judge others charitably. We should banish suspicion whenever charity is possible and should apply the most positive interpretation we can to the actions and intentions of others. This practice of *charitable judgment* is an imitation of God, an expression of faith, and an application of Golden Rule love.

To *think the best* is to interpret others' actions and words in the best possible light, without cynical suspicion on the one hand or naive trust on the other. Yes, we must recognize human depravity and have a realistic awareness that people—even those we may know and trust[1]—can commit evil. But we must also be aware of

1. There are lots of sinners in this world—and too many of them prey on those whom they deem to be weak, vulnerable, and naive. For a long time, the common theory was that parents had to keep their eye primarily on strangers as they protected their kids from abuse. We know differently now. The people

human dignity and of the fact that, very very often, decent people are more mistaken than malicious. While they *may* hurt and *will* offend, they may do so with little ill intent—or even with none at all. So,

> Before you jump to think the worst,
> Believe the best—judge kindly first.

This guideline completes a surprising, counterintuitive communication paradox. Assume bad about yourself, as we saw in the last chapter, and assume good in others, as we are seeing now. Doubt yourself, and give others the benefit of the doubt. Distrust your own intentions, and entrust yourself to God when it comes to others' intentions. Assume that you are wrong, and assume that others are not *as* wrong as their words or deeds might first suggest. This calls us to display not blind trust but an impulse to interpret others' actions and words with as much grace as truth and wisdom permit—to choose charity over suspicion.

SEARCHING THE SCRIPTURES

When Jesus hung on the cross, he prayed, "Father, forgive them, for they know not what they do" (Luke 23:34). Such was the grace of Christ that he interpreted the worst act of history in the best possible light. He minimized the malice of the crucifixion by attributing innocence to his killers.[2] In a similar way, when he entered his hour of trial and his disciples failed him badly, he believed the best about his disciples' hearts, even when their flesh

---

we should watch most closely are those who have worked themselves into our lives and groomed our kids (and us) to trust them and to let down our guard. These people play on our impulse to judge charitably in order to pursue their own evil designs. Due caution is appropriate at all times.

2. Paul goes so far as to say that Jesus's contemporaries would not have killed him if not for the blind spot of their ignorance (see 1 Cor. 2:7–8).

had failed (see Matt. 26:40–41). Jesus's example alone should be all the model that we need in order to respond similarly whenever possible—even toward those who have done us great wrong. And it isn't even alone.

James tells us to avoid partiality—not to prejudge people based on bias or negativity or prejudice (see James 2:1–10; 4:11–12). Mercy is to triumph over judgment. This does not mean that we cannot call wrong *wrong* but that we must not judge based on prejudice or cynicism or self-righteous assessment of others' motives. It is a call to charitable judgment.

Paul picks up this theme when he says, "Love bears all things, believes all things, hopes all things" (1 Cor. 13:7). Humble love believes and hopes all things, refusing to become cynical toward others or to interpret their actions in a negative light unless there is no choice. Love is not naturally suspicious but is ever inclined to assume the best of intentions even when offenses happen.

Paul models this earlier in that same letter.

> I give thanks to my God always for you because of the grace of God that was given you in Christ Jesus . . . *who will sustain you to the end,* guiltless in the day of our Lord Jesus Christ. God is faithful, by whom you were called into the fellowship of his Son, Jesus Christ our Lord. (1 Cor. 1:4, 8–9)

In a letter in which he rebukes the Corinthians for disunity, sexual impurity, lawsuits, the violation of Christian liberty, cultural elitism, drunkenness at the Lord's Supper, gender warfare, the abuse of spiritual gifts, and even some bad theology about the resurrection, he believes better things of them and trusts the ongoing and prevailing grace of God in their lives.

To another scandalously errant church he writes, "I have confidence in the Lord that you will take no other view, and the one who is troubling you will bear the penalty, whoever he is" (Gal. 5:10). Even though the Galatians teetered on the brink of abandoning the gospel (see Gal. 1:6–7), he still believed in them—or, more precisely, in God's grace in them.

Still another example is the author of Hebrews, who, despite the Hebrews' temptation to return to Judaism in open rejection of Christ, writes, "Yet in your case, beloved, we feel sure of better things" (Heb. 6:9).

These are remarkable texts that model how to *think the best* and *believe the best* about others in light of the common, saving, and sanctifying grace of God in their lives. Each of these texts shows that Jesus and his apostles did not measure people by their worst deeds but by their intentions and by what God was doing in them.

This involves *kind and generous interpretations* of others' actions. Martin Luther's Small Catechism says that the ninth commandment—"You shall not bear false witness" (Ex. 20:16)—means that "we should fear and love God so that we do not tell lies about our neighbor, betray him, slander him, or hurt his reputation, but defend him, speak well of him, *and explain everything in the kindest way*."[3] This is truth. Likewise, based on 1 Corinthians 13:7, Jonathan Edwards rebukes a critical and suspicious spirit (which is "a disposition to think evil of others, or to judge evil in them") and commends charitable judgments (which are "a disposition to think the best of others that the case will allow").[4] Given that both of these men were grossly inconsistent in their own application of these principles (Luther toward the Jews and Edwards toward his African slaves), they serve to remind us that biblical love is a lot easier to define than it is to live out.

3. Martin Luther, *The Small Catechism* (St. Louis: Concordia, 1986), answer 61. Emphasis added.

4. Jonathan Edwards, *Charity and Its Fruits: Christian Love as Manifested in the Heart and Life* (repr., Carlisle, PA: Banner of Truth Trust, 1969), 204–5.

WHAT SUSPICION DOES TO OTHERS AND TO US

When we are ruled by a suspicious spirit rather than making a charitable effort to give people the benefit of the doubt, out of love, we create difficult tensions in our relationships. Our cynical distrust of others leads us to assume the worst about them and to be offended by everything that they do, even when no offense is intended. If we have an eye for the worst, we will see it everywhere, all the time—even when it may well not be there at all.

Describing the slavery of his day, Frederick Douglass writes of a "saintly" Rev. Hopkins who would preach kindness on Sunday and then make a point of whipping one or two slaves every Monday. Mr. Douglass comments, in a sardonic tone, "The reader might imagine a difficulty in finding faults enough for such frequent whipping. But this is because you have no idea how easy a matter it is to offend a man who is on the look-out for offenses."[5]

How many relational, marital, parental, racial, ecclesiastical, or theological whippings have we inflicted because we've been on the lookout for offenses? When we look for faults or offenses, we will see—and, even worse, *imagine*—them everywhere, to the great harm of many. We create relationship-crippling vulnerability in others when we impugn people's every action and motive. And ironically, when we suspect others' intentions because we have imagined something wrong in them without proof, we are the ones committing an actual wrong against them.

In addition, suspicion not only harms others but also twists us. Charles Spurgeon writes, "Suspicion makes a man a torment to himself and a spy toward others. Once you begin to suspect, causes for distrust will multiply around you, and your very

5. Frederick Douglass, *My Bondage and My Freedom* (1855; repr., Mineola, NY: Dover Publications, 1969), 259–60.

suspiciousness will create the major part of them."[6] Suspicion twists us into becoming self-appointed word- and motive-police. Soon our lives become continuous undercover operations—adventures in espionage as we seek to root out and expose all the "real" intentions of people's hearts . . . not exactly a formula for trusting and whole relationships.

GOLDEN RULE GRACE

Charitable judgment is Golden Rule grace. Nobody enjoys being wrongly suspected or having their intentions questioned. We don't like it when people overreact to our wrongs and interpret them as being far worse than they are. We want people to give us the benefit of the doubt—and so we should always be ready to give to others what we ourselves want.

This principle has literal street-level value. Imagine that you are cruising at legal speed through the intersection of Main and Church when a blue Chevy pulls out in front of you. It's bad enough that the driver fails to come to a full stop before interrupting your flow. What's even worse is that he takes his time getting up to speed, both costing you the effort of moving your foot from the accelerator to the brake *and* causing an eighteen-second slowdown in your life.

How do you respond? What do you think just happened? Do you think the driver deliberately waited until you were close enough to need to hit the brake, just so that he could tick you off? Did he pause at the corner and mutter with sinister glee, "No, not yet. Don't pull out yet. Give it another second so I can make this guy suffer"? Not likely.

Perhaps it would be helpful to ask some more questions. Have you ever pulled a dumb stunt while driving? In fact, have you ever

6. C. H. Spurgeon, "The Blind Eye and the Deaf Ear," in *Lectures to My Students* (Grand Rapids: Zondervan, 1954), 325.

pulled out in front of someone and made them slow down in the process? And if that driver got upset with you for doing so, did you get upset with him for being so upset with you? If so, why? Wasn't it because you sensed that his anger was unjust? After all, you hadn't intended to cause him inconvenience. You'd made an honest mistake. You hadn't meant to be a bad driver—and you wished that the other driver would chill and give you the benefit of the doubt.

Do to others as you would have them do to you. Think the best. Life will give you plenty of chances to learn how to do this well.

Situation	Thinking the Worst	Thinking the Best
Dr. Jim falls asleep just about every Sunday morning during the sermon.	He is spiritually indifferent!	Maybe his job leaves him exhausted on Sundays, but he is so committed to the church that he comes every week anyway.
Bradley doesn't follow through on a promise.	He is a liar!	Maybe he is overwhelmed right now with other responsibilities.
Elizabeth doesn't say much to you at church, but she talks to others.	She is aloof and cliquish!	Maybe she has a hard time interacting with new people.
Your daughter Olivia doesn't do her chores.	She's a rebellious teen!	Maybe she forgot because she's so busy with schoolwork.

Situation	Thinking the Worst	Thinking the Best
Water cooler talk stops when you arrive.	Your coworkers are gossiping about you!	Maybe they're planning a surprise party at work.
Anthony brings up the race issue again.	He's bitter and just won't let it go!	Maybe he's had life experiences that make this an everyday concern for him.
A certain ethnicity seems to suffer a disproportionate number of arrests.	They're all criminals!	Maybe other factors and/or injustices are contributing to this situation.
A white sister at your church shies away from race conversations.	She's an uncaring racist!	Maybe this is new to her, and she doesn't want to say the wrong thing.
A child acts up in school.	He's a bad and lazy kid!	Maybe he's very bright and is bored because school is too easy.
Your boss withholds a raise.	She's stingy and greedy!	Maybe business is bad, and she's trying to preserve your job.
Pastor Frank doesn't follow your suggestion.	He's out of touch and doesn't listen!	Maybe he knows more about the situation than you do.
Betty disagrees with a pastor's decision.	She's a troublemaker!	Maybe she has an honest difference of opinion.

Situation	Thinking the Worst	Thinking the Best
An international family arrives late for dinner.	They disrespect the value of your time!	Maybe their culture views time differently.
Your husband seems distant.	He's having an affair!	Maybe things are hard at work right now.
Your wife reminds you to get the brakes fixed.	She's a nag!	Maybe she wants your family to be safe.

Our need to think the best meets us daily. There are multiple times every day when we need to mortify our immediate fears, biases, and assumptions in order to embrace the best possible interpretation we can attach to what others say and do.

WHEN TRUST IS HARD

This can feel almost impossibly hard for people—and especially for those who have been repeatedly victimized by others. I think of the sister in the Lord who told me that she had determined never to trust a man again because her father, her husband, and her previous pastors had all abandoned her. Distrust was the shield she had chosen for protection from further hurt. Those who have long experienced the undeniable effects of broken systems and abuses of power face a similar struggle with distrust, as they battle to render charitable judgment toward others. It's hard to believe the best when the worst has happened for so long.[7]

7. One woman writes, "No more than a tiny percentage of women . . . have never been abused by a man. Is it any wonder these women don't trust men or that they equate 'submission' with co-dependence, downright mindlessness, or worse, masochism?" Quoted in Susan Hunt, *By Design: God's Distinctive Calling for Women* (Wheaton, IL: Crossway, 1998), 68. For the full account

I do not have easy answers for these brothers and sisters. I pray for those who are so affected by the vile and violent untrustworthiness of others. I pray that they will be delivered from the real evils of our world and from the outrageous and sometimes enraging effects of those evils. I pray that they may be given a peace that is beyond understanding. I pray that they may at least begin the journey toward charitable judgment by being able to show it first in their close relationships, in their homes, and with a few others here or there, and then might spread that charitableness outward—as far as they are enabled to, by grace.

And I pray that those of us who are not so traumatized by evil will charitably judge those who are—while listening, learning, loving, and lamenting at their side. May we be less dismissive and more supportive—less quick to urge others to "get over" their traumatic experiences and more ready to walk with them through a healing process. As we empathize with their struggle rather than criticize their pain, survivors of various human evils can gain new grace to be able to trust once again.

BUILDING RESERVOIRS OF TRUST

Believing the best about one another gets easier as we create reservoirs of trust in our relationships. On those occasions when Gayline has wronged me, I have been guarded from assuming the worst and been helped to believe the best by the history that we have together—a history in which she has proven her love time and again. Even if she says or does the wrong thing, I can now process that through my experience of her long and lasting love. I can draw from this reservoir of past trustworthiness to help me to believe the best if she offends me today.

And believe me—I try to return that favor. My goal each day

---

of this woman's struggle to trust men, see her anonymous testimony that is included in pages 65–70.

is to live my love for her in such a way that in my moments of sin against her, she will be able to say with good reason, "What Tim did was wrong—but I have all the reason in the world to trust his heart and intentions. He may have hurt me, but I know that is not the true Tim. I will believe the best, because he's proven his love."

Psalm 15 describes for us the authenticity that God commands when we approach him in worship. I believe it also describes an authenticity of character that will go a long way toward deepening the reservoirs of trust in our relationships. We foster trust when our character is consistently blameless and righteous (see v. 2). We enhance that trust in others when we simply tell the truth and do not lie (see v. 2). Their trust deepens further when they see that we do not participate in gossip and unfounded rumor (see v. 3). Our trustworthiness shines forth even more when we make and keep commitments, even when it costs us (see v. 4). And when family, friends, and foes see that we maintain integrity even when money is involved, people will know that we can be depended on (see v. 5).

Replenish your reservoir day by day. Be present. Be faithful. Be there when it's rough. Make it as easy as possible for your spouse or children or fellow church members or cross-cultural friends to believe in your intentions—even when your actions don't measure up.

Perhaps the best way to deepen and fill your trust reservoir is to commit the COMMUNICATE principles that we are learning to your memory and to your life. Do so, and your trust reservoir will fill. Ignore them, and you will have no trust built up for others to draw from when the offenses happen. Resist and refuse this way of life, and you will prove that you need the advice we will discuss in the next chapter.

DISCUSSION AND REFLECTION

1. "Before you jump to think the worst, believe the best—judge kindly first." What are your first thoughts about how worthwhile it sounds to work toward this challenge? How might God's merciful judgment toward you affect your response?
2. Describe a time when someone judged you harshly and uncharitably. How did you respond to that experience, and what lessons might you learn from it?
3. Do you think that everybody has blind spots like those of the people who killed Jesus? How do you respond if someone seems blind to the ongoing effects of racism or to the holocaust of abortion? Does the reality of blind spots make believing the best easier or harder?
4. If you held prejudicial, suspicious assumptions about people of a different color, culture, or class from you, what effect would this have on your relationships with them? How would it affect the unity of your church or workplace?
5. This chapter includes a series of scenarios of people acting in ways that might be read either positively or negatively. As you read that list, did any of the examples mirror your own experience—either with judging others uncharitably yourself or with others doing so to you? Which ones, and how? What are a couple of recent real-life examples you have had yourself with charitable or uncharitable judgment?

CHILL

OPEN UP

MAKE TIME

MEAN WHAT YOU SAY

UNDERSTAND WHAT YOU HEAR

NOURISH WITH GRACE

INITIATE PEACE

CELEBRATE OTHERS

ASSUME YOU ARE WRONG

THINK THE BEST

EXAMINE YOUR HEART

11

EXAMINE YOUR HEART

"What causes quarrels and what causes fights among you? Is it not this, that your passions are at war within you? . . . You adulterous people! Do you not know that friendship with the world is enmity with God?" (James 4:1, 4)

"For from within, out of the heart of man, come evil thoughts . . . deceit . . . slander, pride, foolishness. All these evil things come from within, and they defile a person." (Mark 7:21–23)

"Keep your heart with all vigilance, for from it flow the springs of life." (Prov. 4:23)

Whenever conflict gets a start,
Check for the god that rules your heart.

Mr. Thomas was a good and faithful man who loved Jesus and lived by the Word. He had been in pastoral ministry for around fifty years and had spent his adult life studying the Scriptures and serving people. With a unique blend of truth, vibrancy, mischief, love, and no-nonsense but gentle authority, he ignited a lot of people for Christ—including Gayline and me, who had both known and loved him almost from childhood.

For all these reasons and more, the news of his Alzheimer's hit hard. The thought that a man of such gifting, character, and love would slowly be altered to a point where he wouldn't remember important life events or people or priorities or pleasures was too sad for words. And indeed, the dreadful disease eventually erased nearly everything from his mind and memory. . . . *Nearly* everything.

Time revealed depths in Mr. Thomas that no disease could touch; his true self was etched deeply and indelibly in his inner being. Consider the moment when, after guests had arrived at his home, he disappeared. Unable to find him inside the house, Mrs. Thomas eventually found him in their guests' car, trying to drive it away. No matter what appeals she made to dissuade him, he wouldn't budge—that is, not until she warned him, "Honey, if you take this car, that would be *stealing*." This was the magic word—or, more precisely, the voice of conscience, the voice of the Master he loved. Nothing more needed to be said. Even in his altered state, as soon as he heard that to drive would be to *steal*, he got out of the car and reentered the house. The ancients would say, *Selah*. Time to pause and ponder.

And while you're at it, consider this too. Not long thereafter, the illness so weakened his mind that he could no longer recognize his wife. Mrs. Thomas became a stranger to him—a sorrow that was too poignant even to imagine. And so it was that when he went to bed one night and saw this "unknown" woman in *his* bed, he was appalled. In a show of his faithful devotion to his marriage, he told this woman whom he didn't recognize to leave, assuring her in no uncertain terms that he was a married man. Double *Selah*.

Even though the health of his mind was gone, the health of his conscience and marital devotion wasn't. Mr. Thomas would not consider stealing a car or cheating on his wife, even in his diminished condition, because his heart wouldn't let him. What had ruled his heart for seventy years continued to control his life even when all else failed.

HIS HEART SAID "AMEN"

I once lingered at the bedside of another Alzheimer's patient—a man who was hours away from heaven. He was non-communicative then, though his body was greatly agitated—enough so that the doctors had no choice but to restrain his arms and legs lest he do himself harm. If memory serves me rightly, he hadn't spoken for days; his only "communication" was his frequent straining against the straps that tied him down.

The last time I was with him, I sought to comfort my Christian brother with prolonged readings from Scripture. Isaiah 40. Psalm 23. First Corinthians 15. Revelation 21 and 22. Romans 8. Whatever came to mind I read—and then read some more. As I continued, a slow but growing tranquility stole over his face and then descended and settled throughout the length of his body. In time, his body was still, his face serene, his spirit calm. When my reading was done, much to my wonder, he responded with a strong and earnest "Amen." There he lay, quietly breathing, in peaceful communion with his Maker.

I don't know for sure what the psalmist's words "deep calls to deep" mean (Ps. 42:7). But the phrase can serve as a metaphor for a profound spiritual experience—for that moment when the deep cries and longings of a human heart respond to the deep voice of God (see Ps. 42:1–4, 8). This much I know: that which was deep within my afflicted brother was drawn out when nothing but his Master's own words could reach him. At the end of it all, his heart for God won out, and his lips said "Amen" to his Father's voice.

THE ROLE OF THE HEART

Whether for good or for evil—whether it is the voice of conscience, or the deep longings of the spirit, or the lustful cravings of a covetous soul— what rules our hearts governs our words and lives. This is why the ancient sage said that we should "keep [the] heart with all vigilance, for from it flow the springs of life" (Prov. 4:23).

Paul Tripp calls this "the principle of inescapable influence," saying that "whatever rules the heart will exercise inescapable influence over a person's life and behavior."[1] He gets this straight from Jesus, who said, "Out of the abundance of the heart the mouth speaks. The good person out of his good treasure brings forth good, and the evil person out of his evil treasure brings forth evil" (Matt. 12:34–35). When good fills the heart to abundance, goodness fills the mouth in abundance. But when sinful or excessive desires rule the heart, sinful words and deeds will abound. The heart has an inescapable influence over the life.

Our obedience to God, and our respect for his image in others, result from what our hearts most desire. What we say, how we listen, and whether or not we are willing to chill, open up, make time, mean what we say, understand what we hear, nourish with grace, initiate peace, celebrate others, assume we are wrong, and think the best are all decided by how much *want-to* we have. If we *want to* honor God and respect the image *more* than we want anything else, then that is the life we will choose. If we are struggling mightily to resist these things, then it is time that we examine our hearts in order to find out what our problem is.

WHY WE FIGHT AND QUARREL

Self-reflection reveals that our problem is us. If we are fighting with others, no matter what *their* issues may be, it means that *we* have issues ourselves—heart issues involving spiritual infidelity to Christ. Relationships suffer when we love something or

1. Paul Tripp, *Instruments of Change: How God Can Use You to Help People Grow* (Glenside, PA: Christian Counseling and Educational Foundation, 2000), Lesson 2 , pp. 2–5; and Lesson 3, pp. 2–4.

someone more than we love Jesus and more than we desire to honor God by respecting his image in others.

"What causes quarrels and what causes fights among you? Is it not this, that your passions are at war within you? You desire and do not have, so you murder. You covet and cannot obtain, so you fight and quarrel. . . . You adulterous people! Do you not know that friendship with the world is enmity with God?" (James 4:1–4). Strong passions that are unfulfilled, enflamed desires that are unmet, covetous longings that are not obtained—these are why we fight with one another. We break the rules of respectful communication because we want something that others are not giving to us.

This is Biblical Psychology 101. With penetrating insight, James diagnoses the root of the problem. All our arguments and judgments, all our prejudgments and accusations, all our quarrels and resentments, all our feuds and fights, all our strivings and wars, all our racist ranting and anti-racist rage—these all can be traced to frustrated heart cravings. We want whatever it is that we want—power, pleasure, respect, justice, requited love, control of the remote, a bowl of ice cream—and we're willing to fight in order to get it. James says that whatever masters our hearts that *isn't* God will ruin our relationships.

No doubt he learned this truth from his half-brother, Jesus, who said,

> From within, *out of the heart of man*, come evil thoughts, sexual immorality, theft, murder, adultery, coveting, wickedness, deceit, sensuality, envy, slander, pride, foolishness. All these evil things come from within, and they defile a person. (Mark 7:21–23).

As it is with computers, so it is with human behavior: garbage in, garbage out. Bad input produces bad output. Ever since Genesis 3, moral malware has infected the human heart, corrupting the relational and communication hard drive of our lives. We need some major reprogramming.

EXAMINE YOUR HEART

Since our words and deeds are controlled by our wants—since frustrated desires lead to unrestrained words and relationship meltdowns—we have to examine our hearts. If our god (the passion that is currently ruling us) determines the choices we make, then we need self-awareness to discern the heart idols that are catalyzing our sin. This in turn needs to lead us to repent before God and show humility before others.

> Whenever conflict gets a start,
> Check for the god that rules your heart.

Do you remember our story about Cadan and his mischievous milk version of a Gatorade shower that doused your dinner? Recall how you (his parent, in the illustration) became a fire-breathing dragon and exhaled flame and fury over spilled milk. And consider what stopped your rage: split-second rage control happened the moment that your pastor called and you answered the phone. In one second you would have said that you couldn't help yourself—that you just had to vent. In the next, you became the embodiment of calm . . . a near-miraculous transformation!

The simple answer for why and how you were able to do this is that one desire in your heart yielded to another when the phone dinged. Your heart's lust for anger, which caused you to vent over dinner, changed to a lust for reputation, which made you not want to sound bad in another's ears. One moment you desired an orderly dinnertime and fumed when you didn't get it. The next moment you desired a good reputation and repressed your fury in order to preserve it. *Our desires govern what we choose.*

THE WAY IT WORKS

It's helpful for us to understand the internal dynamics that trigger our angry responses to various situations.[2] In the sequential development of a conflict, *desire* leads to perceived *need,* which leads to *demand,* which leads to *expectation,* which leads to *disappointment,* which leads to *punishment*—or sin. This is super slow-motion footage of an argument. Our heated arguments can go from 0 to 60 in three seconds—but if you slow them down to one still frame at a time, you see the ground that they always cover.

First comes *desire.* I want something. Nothing wrong yet—at least not necessarily. Everybody has wants. I want a day without a headache—something I haven't had for over thirty years. Every day, all day, for more than 11,000 straight days, my head has registered at least a 6.5 on the pain scale.[3] So yes, I really want to be headache-free. Nothing wrong with that.

Your wants will vary. You may want a wife's respect or a husband's love. You may want your way in a decision or for your job to pay more. You may want a quiet evening without family drama or a bowl of ice cream to be hand-delivered by your spouse. You may be hoping for your kids to believe and behave or for that guy in church to ask you out. You may long for a Christian brother to really *get it* when you grieve over the prejudice that you have experienced. You may wish that the Christian sister would not be so angry when she talks about how men have treated her. You may yearn for a Christian man to understand, just once, how sexism has impacted your life. All of these are legit.

Of course, we have plenty of cravings that are sinful all on their

2. I am borrowing heavily here, with some slight alteration, from Paul Tripp, to whom I am much indebted. See Tripp, *Instruments of Change,* Lessons 3 and 4.

3. See Timothy M. Shorey, *30/30 Hindsight: 30 Reflections on a 30-Year Headache* (Shawnee, KS: Primedia eLaunch, 2019).

own—longings to have a neighbor's wife, or to get wasted, or to watch porn, or to exact vengeance, or to dominate and abuse, or to steal just for the thrill of it. There are illicit desires everywhere in this fallen world that appeal to our flesh. But whether it is licit or illicit, *any* desire of our hearts, if left unchecked, can become a bomb in our relationships, a barrier to our communication, and a block to our mutual respect and love.

Second in the process comes *need*. My nurturing of a desire alters my perception of that desire. No longer something I would *like* to have, it becomes something that I *have* to have. Pampered desires, even if they are innocent in themselves, become perceived needs. When desires are implanted and then gestate in the womb of the heart, they develop from being wants into being *needs,* and sinful actions or arguments are born (see James 1:14–15).

It's important for us to see that often the danger in our desires lies not with the desire itself, or even with the thing that is desired, but with what the old saints used to call *inordinate desire*—desire on steroids. "The evil in our desires is most often not in what we desire but that we desire it too much."[4] When this happens, personal desires morph into perceived needs. We begin to think of something that we want as being something that we cannot live without, and the trouble begins.

Third comes *demand*. I turn a perceived need into a "right" that others are obligated to provide for me. When I perceive a desire to be a need, it won't be long before I demand that someone give it to me. After all, shouldn't people around me meet my needs? I'm entitled. They're obligated. I need a bowl of ice cream,

4. Though these words are often attributed to Calvin the Reformer, I cannot find the documentation to prove it. They may be somebody's loose paraphrase of something we know he wrote: "We teach that all human desires are evil, and charge them with sin—not in that they are natural, but because they are inordinate." John Calvin, *Institutes of the Christian Religion,* vol. 1, ed. John T. McNeill, trans. Ford Lewis Battles (Louisville, KY, Westminster John Knox Press, 1960), 3.3.12. To my mind, the paraphrase says it better.

and anybody with half a brain will agree that *somebody* should get it for me.

Fourth comes *expectation.* I assume that I will receive what I believe is rightfully mine. If I need it, then it is my right. And if it is my right, then it's only natural for me to expect someone to meet that demand. What could make more sense? We expect the hand-delivered bowl of ice cream, the respect that we are owed, the understanding that we need, the charitable judgment that we deserve, the justice that we have coming to us, the right-of-way that is ours on the road, the nice weather that we want, the headache cure for which we long. Our hearts are full of expectations, and we count on others to come through for us.

Fifth comes *disappointment.* This point of crisis comes when people don't meet our expectations. When our expectations of God and others are frustrated, disappointment shakes us and rocks our relational world. And, truth be told, only the most mature among us can experience the upheaval of disappointment without some cracks of sin showing up in our relational foundations.

Sixth comes *punishment.* This is when we make sure that someone *pays* for disappointing us. War begins. We punish. And everything from blowing up to clamming up ensues.

FIGHTING WITH GOD (AND ONE ANOTHER)

This process is how people get into arguments—not just with cousin Gary or coworker Gwyneth but also with almighty God. Many people are not on speaking terms with God because, from where they sit, he has been a major disappointment. They have experienced a vertical "want, need, demand, expectation, disappointment" phenomenon because of God's allowance of suffering in their lives or in the lives of others. They are not happy with the God who allegedly wasn't there for them.

At one level, I can see how this plays out. I very much want, and could easily feel that I *need,* my headache to go away. *Demand*

and *expectation* follow as a result of easy, earthbound logic. After all, if God loves me, how could he allow me to suffer for 11,000 and more days in a row? If I start with the premise that a loving God wouldn't let this happen, and if that leads to an expectation that he *won't* let it happen, then I'll be pretty ticked if he does.[5] This is the beef that many have with God, and it's the excuse that they use to shut him out of their lives. Those who know the God of Scripture know that this isn't valid, of course—but try telling some people that. They're fighting mad because, in their view, God has let them down.

And the same goes for how they feel about the guy next door, which is James's main point. We get fighting mad because someone has disappointed our expectations. And now there's fury to pay.

SPIRITUAL ADULTERY: CHECKING FOR IDOLS

Whether it is directed vertically or horizontally, our sin is serious when we get caught in the spiraling vortex of desire that has gone bad. When we want what we want so badly that we are willing to go to war with God or others in order to get it, that *want* is an idol—an in-the-moment heart-ruling god that is *not* God. This is why James rebukes these sinful cravings so sharply:

5. I do not want to trivialize the struggle against doubt and anger that takes place when God allows suffering in our lives. It can be an agonizing journey into darkness, as so many writers in Scripture itself attest. A reading of psalms such as Psalm 77, and many others, reveals that when unexplained and seemingly arbitrary trials happen, and when God seems to do nothing about them, tremendous spiritual conflict can ensue. What we need in such times is to answer and comfort our honest, authentically expressed grief with a restored trust in God. We may experience this trust being restored through fresh experiences of our Father's character, promises, faithfulness, and unfailing love—which are often mediated to us through the sympathy, empathy, and comfort of his people.

"You desire and do not have, so you murder. You covet and cannot obtain, so you fight and quarrel. . . . *You adulterous people!* Do you not know that friendship with the world is *enmity* with God? Therefore whoever wishes to be a friend of the world *makes himself an enemy of God*" (James 4:2, 4).

Those who fight and quarrel to get what they want are spiritual adulterers and enemies of God—and that includes you, when you yell at Cadan for upsetting your desired order by spilling his milk. In pursuit of their own agenda, such people have set themselves in opposition to God's throne and his holy will. James's stern rebuke comes with an equally stern call to repentance:

> Cleanse your hands, you sinners, and purify your hearts, you double-minded. Be wretched and mourn and weep. Let your laughter be turned to mourning and your joy to gloom. Humble yourselves before the Lord, and he will exalt you. (vv. 8–10)

THE WAY FORWARD

James's rebuke and call to repentance chart the way forward for us in our broken relationships and ongoing arguments. Stop. Examine. Repent. Start again. When communication is breaking down and conflict is heating up, we need to examine our hearts. We need to look at what's happening frame by frame so that we can identify, even in the heat of battle, what we want and are fighting to obtain. Then we need to confess that idolatrous desire to God and to each other.

We need to do this right away. We can't wait for the dust to settle. We need to interrupt the argument in mid-battle and ask, "Why am I sinning right now? What is it that I want? What is ruling my heart? What is my god at this moment?" Then we need to repent with sorrow over our spiritual adultery and opposition to God. Once we've mourned and wept before God, we must turn to the image-bearer whom we've been trashing and ask his or her forgiveness, too. After all, we have treated that person as being less valuable than whatever we are craving. Then, once we have confessed to God and sought forgiveness from our verbal sparring partner, we will be in a much better place to restart the conversation with humility and love.

DIAGNOSTICS

We humans tend to be far more given to self-expression than to self-awareness, and we are often unfamiliar with how to read our own hearts in a given moment. In order to overcome this deficiency, we can use the following diagnostic questions to help us to discern our idols in the heat of the moment.

- Am I honoring God right now?
- What is it that I want, here?
- Why am I refusing to let this go?
- In what specific way do I think this person has disappointed me?
- What is the specific offense I am feeling?
- Am I willing to confess my idol in this person's presence right now and ask forgiveness? If not, what idol is keeping me from doing so?

Here is another diagnostic we can use to determine whether a desire has become an idol. We can suspect that this is the case if one of the following is true:

- I am willing to sin in order to get it.
- I feel strong anger, and express it sinfully, when people fail to give it to me.

- I worry and fret over not having it.
- I obsess about it daily.
- I yell at, or curse at, or complain about others for not making it happen for me.
- I get depressed because I don't have it.[6]
- I think more about bringing justice against than giving mercy to those who have kept it from me.
- I grow bitter and start pulling away from those who have not met my expectations.
- I have to drink or smoke or gorge or spend in order to get my mind off it.
- I have to have the last word, and/or I refuse to let it go.

Examining the heart is humbling, holy work. That's why the devil opposes it—and we must oppose him (see James 4:7). It is also why we must embrace the promises of God, because they will enable us to do this work and will bless us on the other side of it (see vv. 6, 10)

A NEW AFFECTION

If our hearts control our lives, then our hearts need to change. For this reason, James commands us to "purify [our] hearts" from the spiritual infidelity of wanting things too much (v. 8). This purification begins with confession, as we have seen already. We need to come clean—to fess up to the idols that are within.

6. Not all depression is due to sin or to sinful desires. Depression can trace to various sources, and needs appropriate care. Edward Welch's book *Depression: Looking Up from the Stubborn Darkness* provides great help for those in or around such darkness of the soul (Greensboro, NC: New Growth Press, 2011).

But confession alone is not enough to change the heart. Idols need to be replaced. This explains James's plea "Draw near to God, and he will draw near to you" (v. 8). Because the heart will always *want* something, or worship someone, supremely, we need to make sure that that someone is God. The best way for us to turn our hearts from idols is to turn them to God (see 1 Thess. 1:9). To cleanse our hearts requires more than renouncing an inordinate desire. It requires that we draw near and embrace a new and surpassing desire in communion with the true and living God. A house that is swept clean of demons but is not then inhabited by Jesus will soon return to its former state (see Matt. 12:43–45). But a heart that is filled with the beauty and love of Christ will keep the demons away. Not only will it love him most, it will love others well.

In the spring of 1975, a girl whom I will call Sally dumped me unceremoniously. Bummed and angry, I became a moping mess and stayed in that pathetic state until July 3. It was then, late in the afternoon, that my moping ended with split-second finality. The transformation involved a complete, instantaneous inner change, which was triggered by my first face-to-face encounter with Gayline. From the very second that I first heard Gayline's "Hi" and saw her smile, I *never* moped over Sally again.

What happened to me needs to happen to us all. It is what one has called "the expulsive power of a new affection."[7] New affections weaken and force out (or expel) old ones. Sighting the beauty named Gayline made me forget all my past romantic affections, and the same can happen in our souls. When the heart is ruled by a new and better affection—by Someone whom it loves more than anything else that it might desire—then its old affections and cravings are dispelled: the idols that weaken our adoring love for the triune God and that poison our love and respect for others.

7. See Thomas Chalmers, *The Expulsive Power of a New Affection* (repr., Louisville, KY: GLH Publishing, 2014).

> A new affection must prevail
> If you would change your sorry tale.

We need to draw near to God, so that our hearts might be satisfied in him, through habits of the heart that are time-tested and proven: Meditation on the Word of God. Prayer before the throne of God. Singing of the praises of God. Fellowship with the people of God. Preaching of the riches of God. Reflection on the attributes of God. Delight in the Son of God. Surrender to the Spirit of God. Devotion to the law of God. Giving to the work of God. Sharing of the gospel of God. Assurance in the grace of God. All these will fill the heart with a devoted love for God.

In this way, we arrive back at the center. The one whose heart is full of God will love him and respect all those who bear his image. Communication with creatures who have been given immortality is best done when we are in living fellowship with the Immortal God—with he "who is the blessed and only Sovereign, the King of kings and Lord of lords, who alone has immortality, who dwells in unapproachable light" (1 Tim. 6:15–16).

When we have seen this blessed and beautiful One with a new and surpassing affection in our hearts, the "springs of life" will flow with freshwater love. Our lips will become fountains of grace, and our ears will be transformed into instruments and guardians of peace.

DISCUSSION AND REFLECTION

1. Try to put into words the twofold process that is summarized here, to make sure you understand it:

   Whenever conflict gets a start,
   Check for the god that rules your heart.

A new affection must prevail
If you would change your sorry tale.

2. Consider the "want, need, demand, expectation, disappointment, punishment" phenomenon in connection with a recent argument you have had. What was the want/need/demand that was driving your anger? Do you need to confess to the Lord and to someone else?
3. Did the diagnostic exercise in this chapter reveal any idols in your heart? If so, what are they, and how might you address them?
4. Think about the concept of "the expulsive power of a new affection." Can you think of other examples besides the one that the author mentioned?
5. If our hearts need a new affection, how do we cultivate it?

CONCLUSION

GRACE TO DO WHAT WE ARE TOLD

"So whoever knows the right thing to do and fails to do it, for him it is sin." (James 4:17)

"Everyone then who hears these words of mine and does them will be like a wise man who built his house on the rock." (Matt. 7:24)

Be diligent, apply it all,
But brace yourself, for you will fall.
You'll stumble when both pushed and tried—
But Jesus for your sins has died.

LIFE ON THE ROCK

Jesus once said, "Everyone then who hears these words of mine and *does* them will be like a wise man who built his house on the rock" (Matt. 7:24; see also James 1:22–25). Pastor Loritts says, "The biblical understanding of the fool is not an ignorant person, rather it is one who fails to act on what he knows."[1] In other words, whether you and I are wise depends on whether we *do* what we have learned. Failure to do what we have learned will prove us to be fools and fakes. But obedience to biblical principles will prove the reality of our love to Christ (see John 14:21, 23–24) and to one another (see 1 John 3:18).

In order to help you to build your relationships on the rock, let me offer a few parting comments about how to apply the principles you have learned in this book.

Application will require you to renew your mind and change your lifestyle through review, study, and prayer. This book has included memory tools to help you carry its teachings with you, but you will still need to review the teachings and make deliberate application of them, since "whoever knows the right thing to do and fails to do it, for him it is sin" (James 4:17).

Application will require you to work on all the communication principles at once. These go together to shape a lifestyle of respect and love. It doesn't work to say, "I'm willing to talk, but I can't be expected to listen, too!" or "I'm willing to say what I mean, but don't expect me to work hard at understanding what you mean" or "I'm willing to open up, but I cannot think about chilling in the process." Wouldn't *that* be fun for everybody? This is an everything-all-at-once commitment—which is another way of saying that it's a lifestyle thing.

Application will reveal your sinfulness. We never know the depth and strength of our communication-related sin until we go to war with it. We are going to fail. We are going to sin. We are going to blow it. When pushed and tried, we are going to fall. But don't be in despair. Grace will prevail!

1. Bryan Loritts, *Right Color, Wrong Culture: The Type of Leader Every Organization Needs to Become Multiethnic* (Chicago: Moody Publishers, 2014), 77.

THE PARDON AND POWER OF THE GOSPEL

That James calls our relational sins murder (see James 4:1–2) as well as enmity with God (see v. 4) means that they are very serious. So much so that you may wonder, "If refusing to communicate respectfully with others and fighting over the things that I want but am not getting from others makes me a functional enemy of God, then what hope is there?" There is hope in the gospel—which is why we need to live cross- and truth-centered lives. For, if we humble ourselves before the Lord, he will exalt us through his grace (see vv. 8–10).

We need daily reminders that God is neither surprised nor irreconcilably put off by our unkind and disrespectful words.

> Since, therefore, we have now been justified by his blood, much more shall we be saved by him from the wrath of God. For if while we were enemies we were reconciled to God by the death of his Son, much more, now that we are reconciled, shall we be saved by his life. More than that, we also rejoice in God through our Lord Jesus Christ, through whom we have now received reconciliation. (Rom. 5:9–11)

The fact that I may have *functioned* as an enemy of God when I argued this week with my wife or kids or boss or friend does not mean that I *stand* as an enemy of God. The gospel tells me that I do not. "Christ Jesus came into the world to save sinners, of whom I am the foremost" is the life testimony of every saint on earth (1 Tim. 1:15). He died to turn his enemies into friends—to make peace between us and the Father. This means that all the enmity I've ever shown toward God when I've fought and quarreled with others has been atoned for. While I have often made war with God, he has always and only made peace with me.

This is amazing love—the kind of love that fuels new affection in the heart, which is the kind of new affection that can expel the old. If we would love God and respect the image, then we will need to think on these things daily. Likewise, we will need to recall that the gospel promises both pardon and power—pardon that reconciles us to God and power that transforms us into his image. He is transforming us through a constant progressive, re-creative, and restorative process that yields growth even when we fail. Armed with this glorious grace, we have every reason for comfort and great hope. For he who has begun a good work in us will not stop until the project is complete (see Phil. 1:6).

Be diligent, apply it all,
But brace yourself, for you will fall.
You'll stumble when both pushed and tried—
But Jesus for your sins has died.
So mourn your sins, and cling to grace,
And get right up—rejoin the race.
Raise up your head forlornly hung,
For God will heal both ear and tongue.[2]

2. See Appendix C for the complete Communication Couplets poem.

APPENDIX A

GRACE AND RACE FELLOWSHIP: PROXIMITY IN ACTION

In chapter 3 we saw that "proximity is a portal" that can lead us into greater racial understanding. The racial divide in the United States (which has similar manifestations in other parts of the world) is not so much a political or perspective crisis as it is a people crisis. We have a crisis of distrust, which, while it is born first out of centuries of oppression and systemic injustice, is also deepened by a lack of quality communication and time-enriched relationships. Only genuine love that leads to listening that in turn leads to more love can mend the wounds. Racial understanding will happen only once we spend extensive and intensive face-to-face time with actual people who, though different from us, are made in the image just as we are.

Global diversity consultant Andres Tapia agrees. "The road to true reconciliation will involve whites coming on our turf, eating our food, listening to our music, and being comfortable as they experience faith, history, and culture through our eyes. It is not enough to come in as a tourist who returns home with souvenirs and a pen pal but rather as someone who has come to be among us."[1] We cannot be relationship tourists. Nor can we "win the race to unity"[2] and overcome racial or marital or ecclesiastical or any other type of relational dysfunctionality, unless we are willing to plan time—and lots of it—to run that race together.

None of this will be easy, of course. But easy has nothing to do with it. The cross on which Jesus bled out and died, in order to reconcile us all to God and to one another, wasn't easy. Love never is. But true understanding, peace, and reconciliation can happen no other way.

GRACE and Race Fellowship is our plan at Risen Hope Church for seeking proximity with those who are different from us—a context in which we can have difficult conversations across racial lines that normally divide.[3] Designed for people to open up and listen up, these meetings have had a profound impact on us all—though we have a thousand more layers yet to peel before we get to the center of godlike love. In addition to these meetings, we encourage consistent cross-cultural fellowship and hospitality. If real relationship, reconciliation, understanding, and love are going to happen, time has to be committed to them. To that end, you may find the following simple guidelines helpful in your own context and for difficult group discussions that you may have to facilitate.

1. Andres Tapia, "After the Hugs, What?" *Christianity Today*, February 3, 1997, 55.

2. See Clarence Shuler, *Winning the Race to Unity: Is Racial Reconciliation Really Working?* (Chicago: Moody Press, 1998).

3. GRACE and Race Fellowship holds between six and ten conversations a year. We meet in large group contexts, in which we learn to value one another's cultures, as well as in more personal settings, such as weekend brunches in homes. We also sponsor events like our annual international Christmas dinner, where folks from about twenty-five different ethnic backgrounds bring their favorite cultural holiday foods and read Scripture and sing carols in various languages. Our goal is gospel unity as we celebrate the person and work of Christ in varied and beautiful ways.

GRACE AND RACE RULES OF ENGAGEMENT

For the purposes of our conversations, we have adopted some brief rules of engagement that amount to an abbreviated COMMUNICATE approach and are even arranged in another acrostic so that we can carry them with us: GRACE.

- ***G**ospel unity.* We recognize that we are all one in Adam (as human beings who are made in the image of God), that we are all equal in sin (and have plenty of guilt to go around), and that all of us who believe are one and equal in Christ (with the blood and righteousness of Christ being our shared and only hope).
- ***R**espectful dialogue.* We commit to honesty, to Golden Rule attentiveness, and to the principle that it is more important to listen and learn than to argue and win.
- ***A**ssumed ignorance.* We function with a conscious humble certainty that in every difference of opinion we are at least partly wrong and partly ignorant. We are not fully informed or all-wise—and therefore we need to learn.
- ***C**haritable judgment.* We make a kind and gracious commitment not to draw hasty, stereotyped conclusions, to question or judge motives, or to interpret people's words differently from what they say they mean.
- ***E**nduring commitment.* Fueled by hope in the power of the gospel, we commit not to quit the process of listening, learning, and loving—no matter how far apart from one another we might feel or be.

GRACE AND RACE MOMENTS OF LIGHT

Our efforts at communication and understanding have gone slowly. We are novices at this, so we boast of nothing. We are not trumpeting some new cultural-awareness program so much as trying some old biblical principles of love and respect. While the results may not be known beyond our local church or ever be featured as national news, they are encouraging to us and are making a difference in how we see one another.

- A young white man tells us why he voted for a presidential candidate who half our congregation believes is out to get them. When he's done, those who are on the opposite end of the political spectrum embrace him. Even though they still don't agree with him, they understand him.
- A young white police officer stands during the height of the recent police shootings and racial tensions and shares why he is a cop, explaining that all he's really ever wanted is to help and protect people. But now he's thought to be a bigot just because he wears a uniform. When he is done, people of various shades stand to applaud.
- A black couple shares an experience they had in the United States' deep south—a traumatic episode with police that was fueled by racist assumptions and could easily have ended badly. And we grieve.
- A "couple of color" shares how neighborhood folks called the police to check them out simply because they were walking the neighborhood after dark. Nobody's ever done that to Gayline and me.
- A young man weeps over how many times he's been profiled—so many times that he has simply come to accept it as the norm. Many cannot relate, but we try to understand.
- A couple from afar explains why they arrive late for events. In their culture it's acceptable to be late if the delay happens because you are spending time with other people. Where they're from, the person in front of you

takes precedence over the person who is waiting for you. Where I'm from, it's the other way around. We never would have understood this difference if we hadn't asked and listened.

- One person thinks that everyone who opposes big government is a tight-fisted conservative who is indifferent to the poor. Another thinks that everyone who favors bigger government is an unthinking, tax-loving liberal. Listening has taught us that very often neither is true.
- One thinks that everyone who favors welfare must be lazy or have an entitlement mindset. Another thinks that everyone who is opposed to welfare is an uncaring Ebenezer Scrooge. Conversations have taught us that both views are a misunderstanding.
- A Puerto Rican friend is grieved because a national leader demeans her homeland with vulgar disrespect—and yes, come to think of it, that would be hard to take.
- A white woman tells us she has been traumatized for years because people of another culture have robbed her blind and repeatedly called her "trash." We understand her angst, even if she's unfair to prejudge many based on the bad behavior of a few.

These are some benefits of real, open conversation. We realize that the racial crises that affect people all over the world will require much more than lots of conversation—but they will never require less. This is where it has to start. In our church, we have only just begun. But at least we are on the journey.

APPENDIX B

A WORD ABOUT PROFANITY

In chapter 8, I referred to the "profanity of belittlement" and stated that when we belittle others, we are profaning the image of God. Few people have an adequate view of profanity in our times, which is painfully obvious from most conversations that last longer than ten minutes. Profanity is irreverence—a trivializing disrespect for what is holy, beautiful, majestic, good, and even terrifying (such as hell and damnation). We are profane when we fail to reverence God's holiness, honor his law, fear his justice, respect his image, or gratefully enjoy his creation.

Speaking through Moses, God said that people would bear their iniquity when they profaned what is holy (see Lev. 19:8). He insists that what is holy be treated that way. The same is true for what is *good*. Through Paul we are told that those "who forbid marriage and require abstinence from foods that God created to be received with thanksgiving" have abandoned the faith and are deceived by demons (1 Tim. 4:3; see also vv. 1–2). Why are these things so bad? It is because "everything created by God is good, and nothing is to be rejected if it is received with thanksgiving, for it is made holy by the word of God and prayer" (v. 4–5). It is not holy to choose celibacy and a list of man-made taboos because you believe that pleasure and fun are bad. Rather, it is profanity—a demeaning of what God has made, has called good, and has intended for our pleasure and joy (see Acts 14:17).

God applies this to the way we treat *people* when he says to Peter, concerning ethnically and culturally diverse Gentiles, "What God has made clean, do not call common" (Acts 10:15). Peter and most of his Jewish contemporaries were guilty of profanity by their "commonizing," or trivializing, of people who were made in the image of God.

Profanity is not merely about the number of letters in a word; it is about the way we treat, talk about, and/or fail to reverence or enjoy people and things that have been created by God. *Profanity is a bad thing not primarily because it talks about bad things but because it thinks badly of, and talks badly about, good things.* These good things encompass all that God has made—including his male and female human creations, who are made in his image (see Gen. 1:26–31).

Profanity is on display everywhere in our hearts and our culture. Study Scripture in order to learn its true nature, and you will find that the Holy Spirit reveals many aspects of God's being and creation that can be profaned—but ought not to be. Christians would do well to consider the following ways in which it is possible to profane the holy—ways in which we have unfortunately been guilty, and to which more could certainly be added—and to reconsider how they participate in our profanity-laced generation.

- Both dirty jokes and marriage-is-bad asceticism profane human sexuality—a wonderful gift that is meant to be received with gratitude (see Eph. 5:4; 1 Tim. 4:1–4; Heb. 13:4).
- Willful, ongoing sin profanes the blood of the covenant (see Heb. 10:29).
- Partiality and cursing profane the image of God in others (see Acts 10:9–16, 28; James 2:1–13; 3:9–10).

- Ascetic legalism profanes food and drink—creations that God says are "good" and holy (see 1 Tim. 4:1–4).
- Idolatry, conflict, and various relational sins profane Holy Communion (see 1 Cor. 10:14–22; 11:17–22).
- Broken vows, stealing, disobedience to God's commands, and flippant cursing profane the name of God (see Lev. 19:12; 22:31–32; Prov. 30:9).

We need to cultivate a more comprehensive understanding of the nature of profanity and to guard against every expression of it in the heart and on the tongue. Once we have identified all the things or actions or people that God describes as being holy or clean or good, we then need to treat them with the kind of respect, gratitude, and joy that they deserve. What's at stake here is much more than the putting off of the sin of profanity. What's at stake is a putting on of respect for, wonder at, awe at, and joy in all that God calls good, beautiful, majestic, and true.

APPENDIX C

COMMUNICATION COUPLETS

Since it's God's image we reflect,
Let us converse with deep respect.

To keep from war while in a spat,
Turn down your anger thermostat.
To keep your heart and spirit closed
Does far more harm than is supposed.
To talk takes time, so try to plan
How much and when, as best you can.
Since being heard depends on you,
Make all your words both straight and true.
To listen, cover mouth with hand
And bend your ear to understand.
The gladness of relationships
Is nourished by your grace-filled lips.
To make the peace you wish you had,
Don't ever go to bed still mad!
Take moments with each human being
To celebrate the grace you're seeing.
That you are wrong you may assume—

And by this give the truth some room.
Before you jump to think the worst,
Believe the best—judge kindly first.
Whenever conflict gets a start,
Check for the god that rules your heart.
A new affection must prevail
If you would change your sorry tale.

Be diligent, apply it all,
But brace yourself, for you will fall.
You'll stumble when both pushed and tried—
But Jesus for your sins has died.
So mourn your sins, and cling to grace,
And get right up—rejoin the race.
Raise up your head forlornly hung,
For God will heal both ear and tongue.

Did you find this book helpful?
Consider leaving a review online.
The author appreciates your feedback!

Or write to P&R at editorial@prpbooks.com
with your comments. We'd love to hear from you.